FIRED
at 57

FIRED
at 57

My Fight for Justice
in Christian Academia

RUTH A. TUCKER

Podium Press
Grand Rapids

CONTENTS

"The Mysterious Case of Prof. Tucker"

Fired at fifty-seven. Not the first time. I was fired at twenty-four. A fresh M.A. degree from Baylor University, now a waitress at an up-scale seafood water-front restaurant right at the bridge going into Wildwood, New Jersey. I had worked my way through college collecting tips, but here I was overwhelmed with too many hot plates (no trays allowed) and too many options for oysters on the pages of a complicated menu. But the tips were good—sometimes, I'm sure, out of pure pity. By the end of the second week I was making great progress. My manager didn't agree. With no warning he told me I would no longer be on the schedule. His decision was final. No apologies. I was shell-shocked. I drove home with a heavy heart and a heavy handbag full of change. The next day I started looking for another job.

I was fired for incompetence, fair and square. There was no gratuitous "god-talk." This volume is devoid of god-talk on my part, though loaded with it from those who fired me at Calvin Seminary. Such god-talk may seem odd to those outside the Christian workplace. Here firings are sugar-coated with the "I've-prayed-about-it" defense. Indeed, if words are taken at face value, my firing was an incredibly holy process, hours upon hours of fervent prayer, God leading every step of the way. At one point I was even accused of not sufficiently appreciating their prayers on my behalf. This whole dynamic in Christian culture is nothing short of spiritual abuse.

So, the reader will search in vain for testimonies of God confirming my actions through prayer. Right or wrong, I don't speak for God. Nor did I as a professor responding to accusations. Likewise, neither my first firing nor my last, was announced with those now infamous words: *You're fired!* But straightforward or couched in god-talk, the words meant the same.

I'm certainly not the first author to detail serious seminary dysfunction without god-talk. In the late 1980s, I well remember the animated faculty discussions at Trinity Evangelical Divinity School. The hot topic centered around George Marsden's controversial book, *Reforming Fundamentalism: Fuller Seminary and the New Evangelicalism*. Gleason Archer, a former Fuller professor took issue with some of Marsden's accounts and was upset that he hadn't stressed God's role in the early years before "liberal" elements predominated. And Fuller President David Hubbard, after reading a draft, wanted Marsden to emphasize "the training of men and women to serve God in ministries all over the world." *How can you write a history of a seminary without emphasizing prayer and God's control from the very beginning?*

Marsden was not surprised by the criticism. In the new Preface, he writes: "The fact that the plot is built around controversial parts of Fuller's early history has led to a number of criticisms that the book failed to focus on other parts of the institution's history." Though hardly a tell-all book, Marsden's work exposes behind-the-scenes details of secrecy and intrigue. Indeed, the section detailing "Black Saturday" is worth the price of the book alone. Among other things, Marsden reveals deep psychological problems among faculty members.

> [President Edward J.] Carnell and [Clarence] Roddy were only the two best-known cases from what over the years was a distressingly high number of serious psychological crises or breakdowns among Fuller's faculty. Carnell's case was the most severe. By the summer of 1961 he had to be hospitalized and was brought out of deep depression only by a major series of shock treatments.

Reforming Fundamentalism is still relevant today amid duplicity and deep-seated cultural clashes in Christian academia. How does a school deal with behind-the-scenes problems? Is transparency an obligation or a liability? Both this volume and Marsden's speak to this issue. Each has a *plot* with a seminary setting, personalities and intrigue. Fuller, founded in 1947, has no denominational backing and no college ties. Calvin, joined at the hip with Calvin University, was founded in 1876 by the Christian Reformed

Church. Fuller grew to some three thousand, Calvin fewer than three hundred. Fuller draws faculty and students from dozens of denominations and independent churches, while Calvin Seminary requires administrators and faculty to belong to one small denomination, the Christian Reformed Church (CRC).

The battle at Fuller was one in a much larger war against *liberalism* being waged in American evangelicalism. My narrative is narrowly focused on my own firing and its subsequent cover-up, but it is part of a much larger picture in Christian academia and this volume includes the stories of others who have been fired amid cover-ups.

The cover-up in my case began very early in the process and is evident on many documents. But it is particularly borne out by colleagues' evaluations before I would be offered a second terminal appointment. Some stated they had no reservations about my being reappointed and brought on tenure track. Several, however, offered very telling comments: "I still don't have any knowledge of any actions or characteristics that warrant what happened to her, so I'm going along with it only because on this matter I trust you guys." Another wrote: "The faculty was asked to place a tremendous amount of trust in the administration with regards to the events surrounding Ruth." Still another: "It has been very uncomfortable and stressful dealing with the mysterious case of Prof. Tucker."

For my part, I wanted transparency. From the very beginning I asked for a review of my case and that all the documents be made available to my colleagues and board members. Administrative bullying, however, thwarted every appeal. Thus, my situation lingered as "the mysterious case of Prof. Tucker" for more than three years during which time I felt deeply shamed and sidelined.

Marsden's cast of characters is large, mine focuses primarily on myself and three administrators: President Neal Plantinga, Vice President of Academic Affairs Henry DeMoor, and Vice President of Administration Duane Kelderman. Marsden is an objective observer. My story is a subjective first-person narrative. But it is hardly without hard factual data. In fact, the narrative could be *fleshed out* by documents alone.

Bringing these memories and documents to light offers a very personal side of a professor's fight for justice. Fired professors, for good reason, do not talk about their shame. It is my desire that this book will prompt others to come forward. My experience will hopefully help to unravel an enigma in higher Christian education. Was my case an extreme and unusual miscarriage of justice cooked up behind closed doors, or was it far more common than we imagine?

Still, the most remarkable aspect of my case is that it is so meticulously supported by documents. Outside independent mediators would come down decisively on my side, and among their conclusions was a most telling comment: "We think that if the seminary goes to court, it will probably lose, in part, because Ruth is well documented."

The independent mediators didn't know that I had already contacted several attorneys asking for assistance only to learn how many firms had connections to the seminary, the college or the CRC, thus turning me down out of hand. Two attorneys invited me to talk, both sympathetic to my cause but independently warning me of my *at-will* employment. They likewise were snagged on the charge against me of "ungodly conduct," insisting that courts don't decide the definition of such. I have since learned otherwise as I detail in this volume. The CRC has a very specific definition that would have been sufficient for me to charge the administration with defamation of character. And the law in this case was on my side:

> In Michigan, a person can only sue for defamation per se if an alleged offending party suggests or implies a person is sexually immoral. Then the aggrieved party can sue for damages without having to prove actual damages.

But not that charge alone. The administrators repeatedly accused me of not adhering to their claims of confidentiality, which the law does not obligate me to do. When President Plantinga charged me with "ungodly conduct" and stamped a *confidential* in capital letters on the memo, I had no obligation to keep that awful slut-shaming to myself. But when he himself repeatedly broke confidentiality codes regarding me, as I point out, he broke the law. So also, when I was threatened and silenced after reporting sexual harassment. But my case was primarily one of sex discrimination, and I clearly establish that no male professor had ever been discriminated against as I had been. Closely related was an astounding lack of gender understanding. A court would furthermore be interested in documents showing repeated threats and intimidation as well as "retaliatory harassment," interestingly, now banned at the seminary. My case is compelling. Like Job, the innocent prophet of old, I cry: *If only a jury could hear my case.* Too late for that, so now readers are my jury.

The immense volume of documents generated by administrators—a gift that just kept on giving—is stunning. Why would they be so foolishly careless? I submit two likely reasons: a religious arrogance lathered with godtalk and secondly, what has been termed the *Dutch mafia*. They were cavalier because they knew they could get away with it. And they did. But if anyone imagines that this can happen only in a small Dutch seminary, they are wrong. My research shows that what I endured is all too prevalent. Indeed, my story relates not only to personnel in academic institutions, but also to all employees in any field. Although my case stands out for its vast amount of documentation, some will read or hear about this book and say it's untrue. But if we've learned anything in recent times, facts matter.

But why wait until now, more than fifteen years after leaving the seminary? I've already told my story in a blog. Indeed, this book offers no new hard evidence. Rather, it expands the blog with personal details and feelings as well as stories of others who have endured similar shocking turmoil in their lives. There are lessons to heed. As Christian schools of higher education encounter culture wars or personality clashes that are potentially tearing them apart, my story is pertinent. And not just for administrators, faculty and staff, but also for students and constituents. It will help to answer the biggest question: Will the controversies be debated and decided in open forums, or will men be huddled in the proverbial *smoke-filled rooms* contriving a cover-up?

> We write to expose the unexposed. If there is one door in the castle you have been told not to go through, you must. The writer's job is to turn the unspeakable into words—not just into any words, but if we can, into rhythm and blues.
>
> Anne Lamott, *Bird by Bird*

ACKNOWLEDGMENTS

To my beloved husband, John Worst, who has read and edited this entire volume three times, I offer my profound gratitude. Far more than that, he has *lived* this volume alongside me years before it was even conceived. Without him, my efforts may never have come to fruition.

It would be tempting also to thank by name the two outside independent mediators who so clearly came down on my side after eight weeks of interviewing the three administrators and me. I do acknowledge them for fulfilling their professional duty—more so for submitting documents that clarify this case.

A special thanks to Patricia Gundry whose books on biblical equality have so influenced my thinking. Having confided in her about the turmoil I was enduring at the seminary, she graciously helped me in launching "My Calvin Seminary Story" online. In the months prior to this, having become aware of my document cache, she asked incredulously: *Don't they know that you're a writer?* Yes, good question. Likewise, her feminist instincts are my own:

I had always been a feminist and egalitarian, before I knew those terms. I'd been raised to be an independent thinker, confident in my ability to do and be whatever I set out to do or be. It came as a shock to me as an older child to realize that some people would want to limit my opportunities solely because I was female.

I would be remiss if I didn't mention Pat's husband, Stan. Having endured an entirely unjust, self-esteem-smashing firing from Moody Bible Institute, he would go on to have a profoundly influential worldwide ministry with Zondervan. The writers mentored and published through his authorization are as numerous as the sands of the sea. I am one of them. My life would be transformed by his enthusiastic support of my first academic book, thus launching my writing career.

This book is a historical overview of my teaching at Calvin Seminary. How could I function in my profession as a historian without documents? Repeatedly, however, administrators, board members and faculty status committee members refused to consider the documents, insisting we want to help you, and the only way we can do that is by looking to the future. Nonsense. Without looking backward there is no way forward.

Without these afore-mentioned documents that tell a terrible story, I would not have been able to write this volume. Thus, to the administrators, colleagues, friends, acquaintances and hundreds of experts in various fields (online and in person) who provided me with documents, expertise and quotes I am grateful.

INTRODUCTION

Unsealing the Environment

In 2000, I became the first full-time female professor in Calvin Theological Seminary's 125-year history. In 2003, a new three-man administration, without warning, removed me from tenure track and gave me a terminal appointment. I was single and fifty-seven. That decision set me reeling. I was stunned and shamed. In the weeks and months that followed, I was sabotaged, sandbagged, slandered, silenced and surveilled, all the while enduring sex discrimination, spiritual abuse, slut-shaming and chicanery of every stripe.

Having exhausted every possible avenue of in-house appeals, in 2005, I contacted the head of the CRC who arranged mediation. I now had the muscle to demand that President Neal Plantinga explain his slut-shaming accusations of "lapses into ungodliness," "ungodly conduct" and other variations of *ungodliness.* Such accusations rumored within CRC circles was a clear charge of sexual immorality. It was critical that he be required to respond in writing. He submitted "notes" (allegedly written some two years earlier) of a meeting with me and Duane Kelderman, another administrator. He claimed he had asked me a straightforward question:

What followed, without pause, was a <u>tirade</u>—a stream of accusations ("of all the sexist tricks, to haul me in here and take me to the woodshed!"), expostulation, and sheer, incoherent rage. I've never in my ministry of thirty-one years witnessed anything like it. All entreaties with entreaty body language

("Ruth, we're trying for a kinder, gentler, ethos. PLEASE help us!) were met with more venom, some of it vulgar (you know where you can shove that!"), and some of it derisive, and all of it motored by one of the single most explosive, out-of-control losses of Christian self-control that I've ever witnessed. This went on for thirty-five minutes.

The accusation is fabricated and false in its entirety. But it does serve as a classic description of a hysterical woman. More on this accusation later, but at first glance one might wonder why the two top administrators would sit and listen for 35 minutes. And, likewise, why was there no mention in any of his emails, memos and letters to me in the next two years after this alleged rage and vulgarity?

It is true, however, that no one has ever accused me of being a nice, sweet, subdued, submissive, godly lady. But unless I were trying to be fired on the spot, I would tend to avoid performing thirty-five minutes of "sheer incoherent rage." Give me the lines to audition for the lead role in the hometown players, and I'll do five minutes of coherent rage. But I would utterly fail at five minutes of incoherent rage, say nothing of thirty-five.

In this volume I seek to elucidate the anguish and turmoil and shame of being fired. Just when I was catching my stride as the only woman professor, I was slapped down. The pain and humiliation at times were almost unbearable. This story needs to be told. Although the focus here is on Christian higher education, a "secular" firing can be equally upending, but rarely is god-talk marshalled forth in support of the decision. Female gender is often a factor, but men also endure awful terminations and suffer from depression and the loss of self-confidence. I'm not alone.

For many people, however, a job firing comes with a settlement. If you will quietly resign and sign an NDA (non-disclosure agreement), we will not tell anyone we fired you. Or, perhaps a severance agreement and references attached to an NDA. Even when there is no settlement, the individual fears being blacklisted. I wanted to "move on" sounds better in an interview than "I was fired." This is particularly true in smaller institutions (as with members of the Christian College Coalition) where there is considerable networking among individuals from different schools. A professor who is fired needs confidentiality; thus, silent suffering is the norm.

All of this makes research very difficult. In fact, there are few, if any, books featuring personal stories. There are, however, online accounts as well as articles in edited books that illuminate my own experience. But as

Colleen Flaherty writes "It's rare for disaffected faculty members within the seminary world to speak out publicly against their institutions."

But why wait so long to publish in book form? I have actually attempted twice in the past, but I had to put my efforts aside. I was not emotionally prepared. Now nearly two decades later I can look back with far more objectivity and the old documents are suddenly shocking again. But why write it up? Just let it go, one friend advised.

When I drove my beat-up green minivan out of the seminary parking lot for the last time, I was sixty-one and happily married. Now in my mid-seventies (and still happily married), I am ready to write this volume. And I'm still hopeful that one day justice might be done. But like so many who have suffered from abuse and discrimination, I know that day may never come. So, I write with the hope that others might be helped and encouraged to tell their own stories. And just maybe those in power might think twice before firing an employee without cause.

Chapter 1 focusses on one late afternoon in January of 2003 when without warning I was given a terminal appointment and removed from tenure track. I was shamed so deeply by the academic dean that at the end of the meeting, midway through the second hour, I was groveling. I pitifully asked: Does anyone have to know?

Chapter 2 features the shocking "smoking gun." After learning that I could see faculty evaluations (without names), I discovered that the summaries the dean used to shame me had been rigged. They were falsified to make me appear utterly unfit to teach. The quotes he read from his written evaluation belonged to two administrators, not fulltime faculty colleagues.

Chapter 3 deals with sex discrimination. Colleagues insisted that a person who affirms gender equality could not be guilty of sexism. Not so. If a female professor ranks as high as her male colleagues on measurable criteria but is judged by a different standard and fired, that is sex discrimination. Case closed. This is precisely what I allege happened to me.

Chapter 4 shows how quickly the administrators moved the goalposts away from alleged awful evaluations to *ungodliness* in all its verbal forms. I tell how I was "slut-shamed" and required to enter a "Renewal Program" to "preserve my dignity." All the while rumors were flying and colleagues didn't want to touch my case with a ten-foot pole.

Chapter 5 brings to the fore women's physical and emotional differences from those of men. I was the only one among administrators and faculty who would ever endure the miseries of menopause with its hot flashes, excessive bleeding, D&Cs, blood transfusions, fatigue and sleeplessness. Colleagues' medical issues afforded good stories, pity and concern. Not mine.

Chapter 6 zeros in on surveillance and psychological testing. When the administrators needed to further bolster their case against me, they began scrutinizing my every move. Petty offenses such as absence from chapel or leaving a meeting early were magnified. They ordered me to submit to psychological testing. I lived in fear.

Chapter 7 identifies the awful ordeal professors endure amid academic mobbing and not just bullying from administrators. Colleagues had endorsed my first reappointment but a year later they seriously faulted me for keeping to myself and not socializing in the faculty room. I should buck-up and take my punishment like a man.

Chapter 8 focusses on a five-page threatening letter from Neal Plantinga because I had reached out to the American Association of University Women for help. I had dared seek justice outside the seminary. Six times in bold print he wrote: "This violation is a ground for termination." The letter would lead to reviews by a board committee and later by outside independent mediators.

Chapter 9 demonstrates conclusively that Neal Plantinga's description of my alleged "ungodly conduct" was a fabricated sexist rant. Drawing from age-old accusations against women's mental stability, it serves as exhibit A for a "hysterical woman." I should not have been surprised that he would stoop so low. But it only added evidence to the administration's assault against me.

Chapter 10 highlights my life outside the Seminary walls. I was free and I found a sense of peace. Opportunities for writing and lecturing opened up. But this is not the endgame for most people. Many face serious financial struggles with no job prospects. For them, I am terribly saddened. I have no 10-point program to make their troubles go away.

I write this book for those professors who have been sabotaged in their teaching professions, perhaps young with families to support or ones nearing retirement afraid of age discrimination. The fear of going public is overwhelming. Like me, most have admitted their *deficiencies*. Without a doubt I own many. All we have asked for is a fair shake—for justice. My own anger and upset has diminished significantly over the years. In fact, I have gone for weeks on end barely thinking about that time of tribulation. But as similar stories of others have been reported in recent years, I have felt compelled to step up and do something constructive. I tell stories of others in each chapter, and to them and all who have been unfairly fired, I dedicate this book.

Does anyone have to know? This was my pitiful question on that late afternoon the academic dean gave me a terminal appointment and removed me from tenure track. I returned home late that night to a cold house, got into bed and wept. During that dark and sleepless night, I could not have even begun to imagine that within days, I would reverse that very question. I wanted everyone to know. I wanted my colleagues to see the falsified summary of my evaluations. I wanted anyone and everyone to see all the evidence. The administrators fought back and would largely succeed in their stated effort to "seal the environment."

For more than three years I was bowed down with shame. It doesn't have to be that way. With this book the shame is gone, the environment is unsealed. I want everyone to know.

> Dump your shame and move on. . . . Those first few weeks after the news descends can be a foggy ride. You'll oscillate wildly through emotions without warning. One minute you might be energized and writing up a to-do list of things you suddenly have time for, like "clean out recycling bins" or "learn to knit." The next, you'll be sobbing. . . .
>
> Leslie Zacks, "Nobody Cares that You were Fired"

1

"Does Anyone Have to Know"

Shame and Self-Doubt

I had a job that I loved. . . . I was fired and I am now unemployed. I feel incredibly ashamed and depressed, to the point that I do not want anyone who might know me to see me. . . . [M]y self-confidence is completely devastated.

Anonymous, "How do I deal with the shame of being fired?"

Late afternoon, January 2, 2003. My first routine evaluation for re-appointment since I had begun teaching in the fall of 2000 at Calvin Seminary. Things had gone well with students and colleagues, and my outside involvement was outstanding: conference lectures, church speaking engagements, book and article publications, as well as several translations of books I had previously written, all of which I summarized and submitted to Henry De Moor, Vice President of Academic Affairs.

What should have been a predictable hour of pleasant interaction quickly turned somber with a series of bewildering accusations. He began with generalizations about my not having fulfilled certain obligations, including my not becoming familiar enough with the CRC and other seemingly less than incriminating shortcomings. I explained that I had fulfilled those obligations while he insisted, I could have done much more. He was not reading from notes, rather offering an overview of matters that troubled him. I recall asking two or three times why he hadn't advised me of

1

his concerns earlier. He responded that, due to his busy schedule, he had only recently begun working on my reappointment evaluation.

He then began reading from the text. The first lines were innocent enough, thanking me for submitting my own self-assessment that included a positive outlook for the future. He then turned to student evaluations, slowly reading his very negative summary. I was baffled. I always studied my student evaluations. More than that I had made an appointment with the previous academic dean at the end of my first year. I had pointed to some adverse remarks. Looking them over, he emphasized all the positive comments, saying it would take time before some of the male students would accept a woman on the faculty. I left his office knowing he had my back. Unfortunately, he did not remain at his post to serve in the new administration.

Though entirely unprepared for Henry's negative summary, I was fully capable of holding my own in challenging discussions. But it quickly became clear that this was not a discussion. It was a well-prepared indictment. No allowance for interruption, apart from what I scrambled to insert in self-defense. But my sentences were silenced by his false claims. From his evaluation, he read that students "proceed[ed] immediately to single out" such things as "lack of direction." They "expressed some frustration with class time." Moreover, "Students were unsure. . . . Further, students expressed some frustration. . . . Many suggested. . . . Many commented . . . . they would like more theological underpinnings."

He read a few good comments as well, but from his remarks, it was clear that those did not have the weight of the many negative ones. He then moved on to students he had talked with personally—reading and making comments about them. These were comments I couldn't check out and were clearly the most disparaging of all. It had never occurred to me that he would stop students in the hall or invite them to his office to evaluate me.

I began to realize that he was suggesting that I was unfit to teach at the seminary. His numbing charges continued. I kept trying to insert observations I knew to be true, but he had the *facts*. When I asked him to further explain his more generalized comments, he said he would give me a copy when he was finished and that I would find it very comprehensive and clear. He told me I should read it and pray about it. If I still had any questions, I could make an appointment to see him. He indicated that he did not want interaction at that point. I recall feeling confused and traumatized, knowing something was very wrong. It was almost as though the room had grown cold, a dark shroud engulfing me.

Menacing Quotes of Colleagues

Henry then moved to the next section of his evaluation and began generalizing problems I was allegedly having with my colleagues. I was struggling to understand. What was he referring to? Again, I tried to ask questions, but he insisted this was not the time for that. As he continued, I kept wondering where this was leading. He had frequently been in the faculty lunch room as colleagues sparred and joked with each other. Why wouldn't he have observed these collegial problems and helped facilitate a remedy? That I wasn't aware of such problems might be excused. But he was the dean and he had been a faculty member for many years.

Why hadn't he helped me? My mind was muddled. Then he began quoting opinions of colleagues. Some trivial. But then the quotes became alarming. These were no longer Henry's observations, but colleagues' actual words. I couldn't believe what I was hearing. Why would they have said such things? I was speechless. How could I face them in the hallway? Their comments were thoroughly demoralizing: "concerns about Ruth's character," about her "competence," about her "theological fidelity," about "her ability to relate to students." In summation, he quoted one of my colleagues: The "faculty lacks confidence in Ruth." He was reading directly from their evaluations. How could I ever easily laugh and joke with them again?

My mind was racing. I was attempting to process Henry's allegations and at the same time I was hearing voices—voices of colleagues. Voices of condemnation. Censuring me in broad strokes. Had I misinterpreted their outward camaraderie? They had treated me as an equal—at least that is what I had so desperately wanted to believe. How could I have been so naïve? I had no idea how deficient they thought me to be. The quotes continued. Lack of "pedagogical competence," lack of "commitment to the Reformed faith," and still again "reservations about her character."

I'm a strong articulate woman. But now I was completely cowed with no comeback. How could I even begin to answer? Students' comments, yes, I had proof. But these were the very voices of my colleagues.

There is a point that pushes a person to the edge. I had reached that point. I wanted more than anything else to become invisible—to somehow disappear. Some of the psychology pundits counsel the shamed individual that life always gets better. Just think positive thoughts. Perhaps good advice in the long-run but in the moment, it doesn't work. How does one appear upbeat while being so thoroughly shamed?

Had I been having positive thoughts instead of a meltdown, I might have remembered Jack Handey of Saturday Night Live. He was a big hit, known for his *Deep Thoughts.* "If you're being chased by an angry bull," for example, "and then you notice you're also being chased by a swarm of bees, it doesn't really change things. Just keep on running." I laugh and even as I'm writing this, I can hear his slow, therapy voice. *Just keep on running.* Actually, in my case, not bad advice. But on that fateful night in Henry's office, the only humor—if there had been any—would have been very black indeed.

If I been thinking straight, I would have known that I would survive this trauma. But I was a mess. I could barely process what I was hearing. Henry was watching me closely. He had to know how terribly distraught I was. No hint of consolation on his part. He said nothing like, *come on, Ruth, this isn't the end of the world.* Of course, it wasn't the end of the world. But any such comment would have been entirely premature. He knew very well that the worst was yet to come. He hadn't even begun to finish reading his evaluation.

The Clincher

Even before he arrived at his conclusion, I was feeling shamed as I had never been shamed before. Shamed by the Academic Dean who I had assumed was my friend and supporter. No warning. No offer to help me reverse his apparent estimation that I was a truly terrible teacher and colleague. So bad that he had no choice but to continue reading. He glossed right over the evaluations of board members who I would later see had written very positive things after having visited two classes unannounced. For a moment I felt relieved even as he quickly moved on to some routine criticisms he had figured out on his own. Then, more than an hour into the ordeal, he came to his knock-out punch. He slowed down and read very deliberately:

"I will recommend to him [President Neal Plantinga] that you be extended a one-year terminal appointment." In case I might not understand those words, he explained: "A terminal appointment means that your service to Calvin Theological Seminary will end when the 2003-2004 academic year is completed." As much as he had been building up to this for more than an hour, the words were shattering. In one full-swoop, I was given a terminal appointment and removed from tenure track. It was a "career-stopper," an outside independent mediator would later say.

I was astonished. I could not believe what I was hearing. Even at that point, I defended myself. But I was so taken aback that I was virtually helpless. He had the documents on his desk. He was prepared. I was filled with self-doubt. I had been deceiving myself. I truly was a bad teacher and colleague. I should have realized students and colleagues didn't like me and wanted me out of the seminary. The other professors were far better than me. I had to go. I was beyond saving. Henry kept talking and re-reading and explaining.

But why didn't you warn me? I was pleading. I was begging for help. He insisted he was surprised himself. He simply hadn't realized how dire the situation was. He kept going on and on. I couldn't understand his reasoning. Was I really so dreadfully incompetent that his only option was to fire me? This was Henry after all. We had laughed and joked together in the faculty lunch room. I had freely talked with him about rescheduling courses and other routine issues. Never a hint of displeasure. Now this. How could it be?

My Pitiful Self

It is worth pointing out that, as a historian, I had been eager to learn about old-time Calvin Seminary. Among other things, there had been a very serious dust-up in the 1950s when some *liberal* faculty members were dismissed. Also a story about a professor caught going to a movie theater, claiming he had simply stepped inside the door of the theater to adjust his false teeth. It was a sorry excuse. He was sacked. Had I thought of him while I was being demeaned by Henry, I might have felt his pain.

I had plenty of excuses myself. But self-doubt had taken over. I had become convinced of my utter failure and incompetence. My mind, however, was streaming ahead. What would people think? The humiliation was overwhelming. My brain was fried—no other term captures my psychological state. Then well into the second hour, in a quavering voice, I asked: *Does anyone have to know about this?*

I look back and ponder my pitiful self. That's not me. I'm a fighter. Who was that pathetic person asking such a senseless question? *Does anyone have to know?* That inane question, however, changed the dynamics. In a sudden reversal, Henry took pity on me. He sympathetically said, *no one else will have to know.* We can keep this confidential. Of course, he would have to report back to Neal. But nothing, he told me, needs to be said to your colleagues.

Nothing needs to be said. From that moment Henry almost turned into the pastor he once had been, offering words of consolation. His speech slowed and softened. He said he was sorry that the situation had come down to this. He felt bad but he simply had no other choice. I recall feeling soothed by his words. After all, it was Henry. He had always been kind to me. I felt assured that he would not tell anyone about how worthless I was. Nobody would have to know I was fired. Maybe he would even let me resign. Somehow, I might be able to get through this. I wouldn't know it at the time, but these few minutes were what experts call "trauma bonding." A person is beaten down emotionally and she begins bonding with her abuser.

When he was finished speaking, I remember very clearly standing up and hanging on to my chair for fear of collapsing. In fact, I thought he might have to reach over and break my fall. He had come around from behind his desk. We were that close. His final words of consolation: "Would you like me to pray for you?" This was Henry. He was offering to pray for me. I was a weak and faltering sinner. Prayer was a good thing. But despite my numbness and lack of clarity, I somehow had the presence of mind to say no.

Does anyone have to know? I look back over nearly two decades and smile. If Henry had needed more reasons to fire me, he could have added that dumb question.

Alone in a Dark Night

After leaving Henry's office, I walked slowly through the dark hallway, making two right-angle turns to get to my own office. Colleagues had hours earlier left for the day or were still away on Christmas break. I closed my office door sat down in my chair and wept. There was no way that colleagues wouldn't find out. What would I tell people? How would I ever get another teaching position? How would I earn a living? Would my publishers ever again consider a book proposal? What would my peers from other institutions think?

I was broken. I was so terribly humiliated. I would have to tell my son Carlton. He would keep the secret, too ashamed himself to tell anyone. But he had been so proud of me and my teaching and writing. Now even he would be mortified. Shame. It was overwhelming. In "The Pain of Shame," Psychologist Carrie Wilkens writes:

> The problem with shame is that it is a motivator loaded with problems because it is fear based. And instead of differentiating the behavior from the person, it makes the whole person bad, it sends the message that "you are bad" . . . "you aren't worth helping", "you can't be helped", "you are a lost cause", and "we need to be rid of you."

I sat at my desk, waiting maybe twenty minutes before I had the courage to turn on the light and open the envelope with my copy of Henry's reappointment evaluation. As I read, my initial confusion slowly turned to disbelief. There were no statistics. I hadn't even thought of that as he was reading his evaluation of me. If I were such a terrible teacher, why hadn't I been rated alongside my colleagues? I still had on my desk a duplicate set of student evaluations, including statistics, from a fall-term course. Had Henry cherry picked negative quotes from my previous two and a half years of teaching and ignored obvious statistics?

And where were the positive quotes? Sure, he included a few, but the vast majority were critical. I looked down at my actual set of evaluations. A significant majority were positive. Then I looked at the statistics. There was no way to set them alongside and compare them with my colleagues, but statistically my numbers were respectable—my lowest two areas were on grading issues. True, students had complaints about their grades. In fact, a recently retired professor in my department had a reputation of never giving lower than an A-. Not me.

I stayed in my office until after midnight. Before leaving I stopped by the copy room to pick up my printed, well-argued, fact-filled letter of protest I had just written to Henry. Then I walked to the faculty room and put it in his mailbox. That was the beginning of the defense I conducted for the next three and a half years, sufficient enough, with the help of colleagues to put off my termination until 2006. I had been removed from tenure track and would remain so for the duration of that time.

When I arrived home that bitter January 3rd morning, the house was cold. I hadn't eaten since lunch but I had no appetite. I got in bed but I didn't sleep. I cried. I was so ashamed. The voices of Henry and my colleagues ringing in my ears: "You are bad," "You aren't worth helping," "You can't be helped," "You are a lost cause," and "We need to be rid of you."

Henry did not actually say those very phrases, but I felt he conveyed the exact meaning. I was bad, so very bad that the school must be rid of me. I wasn't "worth helping." If I had been, he would have gotten help before he terminated me. Indeed, during the months that followed, I learned that another faculty member who, unlike me, had received low student evaluations, was offered training from a pedagogical specialist. The male colleague was "worth helping." I was "a lost cause," and Henry's voice kept ringing in my ears: *we need to be rid of you.*

Colleagues Weigh In

I returned to my office the next morning. The halls were quiet. Classes had not yet begun and most of my colleagues were still away. In the afternoon, however, a colleague stopped by my office, asking what I had been up to over Christmas break. I tried hard to act normally. But then he asked what I was working on. My student evaluations and other papers were still laid out on my desk and counter. I started in on a lame excuse and then I choked. He was a friend. There was silence. Then he asked what was wrong.

I didn't want to tell him. I didn't want anyone to know. He sat down in a chair. I said nothing. What's wrong? Now he acted concerned. Silence. I sobbed as I spilled out the story. He refused to believe it. What are you talking about? This can't be true. I read to him Henry's conclusions, and told him how I had sent a letter with statistics proving my student evaluations were good. He said that he only heard good things about me from students. Then I told him how bad the faculty evaluations were. He was astonished. That can't be so, he said. *We're all glad to have you on board.* He was shaking his head in disbelief. He asked to see Henry's evaluation. After perusing for a few minutes, he said: *I can't believe the faculty would tear you down like this.* His next words were low-keyed but intense: *You know you have the right to see them, don't you?*

My colleague's words had encouraged me, but I was still very fragile. *Does anyone have to know?* Why would I have even asked that question? I asked because I was internalizing everything Henry had said. "You get the message from your community that you are bad," writes Dr. Carrie

Wilkins, that you "deserve to be punished, rejected, abandoned or humiliated." I had been thoroughly shamed by Henry with far more shame to come in the following years. I have now read dozens of stories of awful treatment of professors when they were fired, but I've never encountered one that was so filled with shaming as was mine

It is very difficult for anyone—not just women—to explain being fired. Shame is a huge factor. But such shame is often hidden. A strong individual's instincts are to cover up—to hide her pitiful, sniveling self. I was a woman entering a male seminary world. So also was Meghan. She was not a professor but like me she would be deeply shamed by a seminary administrator. She would only admit it years later.

Megan's Story of Shame

"I remember feeling very ashamed." These are the haunting words of Megan Lively when she was recently asked about a sexual assault that happened many years ago when she was a seminary student. She had managed to go on in life. But after nearly two decades she was confronted by her husband on another matter and for the first time revealed to him what had happened. Although they had been married most of that time, her shame was so damaging that she had been unable to tell him. His first words: "You were raped." She wasn't sure. Was she the one at fault? She feared she was not remembering things correctly.

With her husband's encouragement and with the help of others, she was able to check the records of Southwestern Baptist Theological Seminary. The documentation of her report was still there. Soon word got out. Not long after that, amid the many sexual assault charges facing the Southern Baptist Convention, she was asked to speak publicly about what she had endured. But she was fearful and mortified—the details too raw to even speak the words. She did her best, however, telling how she had been dating a fellow student for only a few weeks. One night he had shown up at her door and she allowed him to come in—or maybe he pushed his way in. Then he raped her. She reported the assault the following morning to the student affairs office, but was immediately sent to President Paige Patterson.

In his office it was almost as though she was being raped again. There was no woman she could talk with, and he wanted all the details—all of the scintillating details. Worse than that. It was her fault. Why did she let him into her room? She was as sinful as he was. He told her she should forgive the young man. One last warning: *Do not report to the police.*

Because of her ability to locate the original report of the assault and because of her agreement to go public, and because of other awful reports relating to Paige Patterson, her public testimony helped to achieve one very positive result. Patterson was forced to resign as president of the seminary. So, some might say he got his dues. But for Megan it wasn't over. There was more shame to come. Many individuals, including some of her own relatives, were furious. They were convinced she was following in the path of the *liberal* #MeToo movement. But, in fact, she was being shamed by some in that very movement because she was anything but a feminist. She allied herself with ones who oppose equality for women in ordained ministry and in marriage. She felt battered from both sides.

The facts are this. One night in 2003, Megan Lively was raped by a male student. The following morning, she was verbally assaulted by Paige Patterson. Patterson shamed and blamed her for an awful assault, warning her not to report it to law enforcement. My case was entirely different. But I can even today almost feel the agony of Henry's verbal assault on the night of January 2, 2003. For Megan: *Do not report what happened.* For me: *Seal the environment.* For each of us the foul coverup had begun in earnest.

Moving Beyond the Night of Shame

Feelings of shame would become even more intense as the administrators leveled new charges against me. I was not fired on the spot, but my feelings of shame and being bullied would continue to the end of my final terminal appointment. My fighting spirit began to return, however, before midnight of that very day. But it would compete right alongside my shame even after I began receiving support from colleagues—the very colleagues Henry quoted, the colleagues who allegedly had deemed me unfit to be one of them.

Less than two weeks after I was terminated, one of those colleagues asked me to see Henry's evaluation and other documents. He quickly realized there was something very sinister going on. He later gave me a copy of the letter he had written to Henry and Neal, including this excerpt:

> I cannot imagine that any man with her credentials, track record, and faculty recommendation would not get reappointed in a regular way. . . . I find all of that incredible. No, it is not incredible it is perverse. Can I remind you

of how traumatic this has been for Ruth? How shocked she was by Henry's initial meeting with her, a meeting that told her she was fired. Her shock and the subsequent profound hurt at being sandbagged by people she thought she knew. . . . This hurt has been devastating. . . . I say the following as a friend and colleague. I think you guys made a grave error.

It was another colleague who had alerted me that it was my right to see faculty evaluations. That fulfilled request would uncover the *smoking gun.* Only then did I realize that had I not made the wrong person mad, I might not have been fired.

We carry a lot of baggage about the idea of being terminated from a job. We think it's a mark of shame, but it isn't. Most people who are terminated (as opposed to getting laid off) didn't get fired because they stopped coming to work. They didn't steal anything. They did something far worse: they made the wrong person mad.

Liz Ryan, "The Ten Best Things About Getting Fired," Forbes.com

2

The Smoking Gun

An Academic Dean's Dishonest Evaluation

The White House released the subpoenaed tapes on August 5. One tape, later known as the "smoking gun" tape, documented the initial stages of the Watergate coverup [that Nixon] . . . had approved plans to thwart the investigation.

Wikipedia

Back in the summer of 1974, I was spending a lot of time nursing my newborn son and watching the Watergate hearings. Within weeks after his birth, the "smoking gun" had become common usage in the American lexicon. The smoking gun in my case was proof of shenanigans to deny an honest outcome in my reappointment process.

Despite my wilting in shame on that fateful night in Henry's office, I was at least subconsciously aware that something was seriously amiss. I had repeatedly asked him why he hadn't warned me. But even as the shame rained down, his excuses rang hollow. As I later read his evaluation and my own student evaluations lying on my desk, I became convinced that he had sabotaged me. But why? I was utterly confused by the cruelty of it all.

In the days that followed, I vowed to get to the bottom of what was happening to me. I had two significant disadvantages. I was a woman and an outsider. Simply stated, I wasn't one of the *good old* boys born and raised in the CRC. What happened to me could never have happened to one of them. They would have immediately banded together if someone from above had tried to take one of them down (as actually occurred some years later). My greatest asset was word from a colleague that I had a right to see faculty evaluations. With those in my hands the smoking gun emerged—and not just one shot fired, not by a long shot.

Faculty Evaluations

On January 7, 2003, I would receive a revised Reappointment Evaluation from Henry, as well as typed copies of all faculty evaluations. I had expected him to comply with my rightful request for the evaluations, but why would he revise his own evaluation that he had only five days earlier defended so forcefully? In fact, one sentence near the end of his original evaluation remained identical in his revised version: "This, Ruth, is as fair and objective a summation as I can deliver based on the wide variety of evaluations received." How could two very different evaluations both be "as fair and objective" as he could deliver? Something very suspicious was going on.

The changes related to his overview of faculty evaluations where my request to see them caught him up short. Now, instead of just three short positive quotes from colleagues ("good fit," "a breath of fresh air," and "proven ability as a writer and researcher"), he noted fifteen—an increase of, let's say, not merely 100%, but of 500%. Or, turn it around and we find that his first evaluation unfairly showed only one fifth the number of favorable faculty evaluations that should have been noted. That amounts to a staggering amount of smoke from the first shot of the gun. Henry, mind you, was not sloppy. He was a very detailed and competent individual.

But the next shot, leaving billows of smoke, followed immediately after. Only two of those evaluating me concluded that I should not be reappointed—only two. And, shockingly, when I compared their statements with Henry's quotes, I saw immediately that these two were the negative quotes Henry had focused on, particularly the one identified as #17. Indeed, #17 was given nearly 40% of the lines quoted on Henry's original evaluation with quotes from only seven colleagues. Thus, the voice of #17 counted exponentially more than that of any other individual. Still, Henry repeated his one-sentence paragraph: "This, Ruth, is as fair and objective a summation as I can deliver."

We set the mystery of #17 aside for a moment to consider student evaluations.

Course Evaluations

I responded to Henry the very night of my termination with statistics and quotes from student evaluations. But curiously he had sought out students who presumably had not submitted evaluations. A *curtesy*, I assume, to the only woman professor. One of these students proceeded to "complain bitterly" about me and "she had heard many similar complaints from others." He concluded, "It should be obvious, Ruth, that they raise some serious concerns." But with actual written evaluations I had proof, not just Henry's verbal claims. I had the documents on my desk. In the letter I sent him that very night, I included statistics and a sampling of positive quotes to balance his very negative slant and made it clear that they were all from different students:

- "Your [sic] the best professor I had in seminary. You know what I think; other professors should follow your style of teaching. You're organized, well prepared, and so knowledgeable. . . . Thank you!"
- "Appreciate her willingness to help me. . . ."
- "Good job teaching. RT knows a lot about history & missions."
- "I liked this class—I have a greater love for those who have gone before—Good to hear the other side of the characters & personal lives."
- "Professor Tucker showed genuine interest and often excitement for her lectures, adding many interesting sidenotes of contrasting viewpoints. I also appreciated her continual comparison to events of church history to the church today—made appropriate challenges."
- "I think this class really provided good useful and meaningful [sic] for church history survey & appreciated Dr. Ruth A. Tucker's academic high quality."
- "Overall, I learned a lot and grew spiritually and intellectually in this class. Thanks. Great class."
- "Your honesty and transparency are refreshing. I also appreciated your ability to lead class discussions. Great job."
- "I have thoroughly enjoyed the class & I give credit for this to the professor who made it fun, engaging and formative."
- "Textbooks! Super duper! Wide range of material was also great. Thanks for being a caring and passionate teacher."

Henry knew that I was a good teacher and that I was well regarded by my colleagues. He, nevertheless, purposely misrepresented both student and faculty evaluations and terminated me. He did so even though he acknowledged that both board members who visited my class unannounced were "manifestly positive in their evaluation of [my] teaching." One might think he wouldn't have dared to fire me with such positive evaluations from trustees. But there's an open secret in small schools like the seminary: the main duties of board members are financial support and rubber-stamping the agenda of the president. The very trustees who evaluated my class ostensibly let him fire me without objection.

Henry had stated that "Analyzing student comments turns out to be a daunting task." True. How does anyone *analyze* two and a half years of quotes? Statistics obviously offer a far more accurate overview, particularly when set alongside those of other faculty. But he didn't want an accurate overview. Only administrators are privy to such overviews—that is, unless a professor receives a copy by mistake. Just months after Henry had claimed I was "significantly below the faculty averages" on student evaluations, I received a set of evaluations for a spring-quarter course I had just taught. He was right. My heart sank. The evaluations were not good. One more punch in the gut. But then as I read them, I realized the comments were untrue and didn't even fit the course.

As it turned out, the evaluations had been sent to me with my name on the envelop, but inside, the course number was wrong. These were not for my course but rather for one taught by an esteemed and tenured male colleague. I returned the evaluations to Henry's assistant, and explained the situation. The next week I received the correct set of evaluations, along with an overview of all courses that had been offered that term. Someone had inadvertently made a big mistake. I was not supposed to have such a document. Out of the sixteen professors evaluated, I was second to the highest. A junior colleague who had just been promoted was at the bottom.

If I'm tempted to crow about my student evaluations, I might have further support from a recent article in *Inside Higher Ed*, by Colleen Flaherty, titled "Even 'Valid' Student Evaluations Are 'Unfair'" (February 27, 2020). The study found that professors teaching "unpopular required courses" (true in my case) and those facing "gender bias" are disadvantaged:

> [T]he study finds that these evaluations are deeply flawed measures of teaching quality. . . . [and] could disadvantage faculty from underrepresented minority groups or punish faculty members who teach unpopular required

courses. . . . They note—rightly—that their field has faced concerns about gender bias, including in student evaluations of female professors. . . .

Henry had purposely misrepresented my student evaluations, as he had in summing up faculty evaluations. Even though I had sent him a letter showing otherwise, he let his negative summary stand in his revised version. What was his motivation? Why would he do this to me? That has always been the foremost question colleagues and others have asked.

Even while I was in Henry's office on that fateful night, I at least subconsciously realized that my termination was not Henry's decision alone, rather one made by the three-man administration. Henry would never have come up with such an unsettling conclusion on his own. He was my friend. He was a regular at lunch time in the faculty room. (The other two were not.) He was part of the fun and interaction. We all agreed, however, that he was low man on the administrative totem pole. What I had heard that night in Henry's office, I quickly understood, was the decision of the other two administrators. Henry was assigned the dirty work.

Most people "get fired" writes Liz Ryan, because "they made the wrong person mad."

The Mystery Administrator #17

What if it turned out that #17 was not even a faculty colleague, rather a member of the three-man administration? That would be a very underhanded and troubling development. And what if the other individual (#7) who recommended I not be reappointed was also an administrator, albeit lower level? In Henry's revised evaluation of me, he had added an interesting sentence: "It is not commonplace to have two members of the faculty oppose a reappointment." This presumably was supposed to add some weight to his decision to fire me. But were they actually faculty?

Regarding the "two members of the faculty," #7 was easy to identify. No one else would have faulted me the way he did. He was in charge of determining student preparedness for ministry in the CRC. Professors were assigned students to interview and to help collate their bulky files. I had no background in the CRC and, unlike my colleagues, had not graduated from the seminary. Not having been tutored, I often consulted with #7, no doubt asking too many dumb questions. But I dutifully interviewed students and summarized their lengthy files. My faculty colleagues would not have known—or cared—about my deficiencies in this area. They had their own student files to assemble, often complaining about how time-consuming the process was.

The author of #17 (unlike #7), however, was malicious. His identification would become so obvious that he might as well have scrawled his signature across each page. In fact, all of the negative comments supposedly from *faculty colleagues* that Henry read to me (as quoted in the last chapter) came from this one individual, #17. When I read his actual evaluation, it was worse than Henry's cherry-picking from it. For example: "I am bothered by Ruth's lack of leadership at the denominational level." Denominational leadership was never part of my job description. I was hired to teach at the seminary, although I did sit on committees at the nearby CRC headquarters. But with his utter disparagement of me, why would he be *bothered* by my lack of denominational leadership?

He continued: "I often find Ruth to be excessively conformist to the predominant faculty ethos, especially when that ethos is negative." In a later chapter I will discuss surveillance of me. Here his statement is relevant because in the previous sentence he had stated, "She says very little in faculty meetings." So how would he know I'm excessively conformist unless he watched me during faculty votes? And presumably majority votes were deemed negative if they didn't go his way. Very early in this game, I was blamed for the "faculty room ethos"—perhaps like a wicked witch who joins the faculty, mixes her brew, magically waves her wand and turns collegial conversation sour.

Some two years later, after I had informed the outside independent mediators that I was certain that Duane Kelderman had written #17, one of them, in a follow-up session with just the two of us, asked Duane directly if he had evaluated me. He admitted that he had. Only two had opposed my reappointment so it was hardly a surprise since he had already made a strong case to the mediators that my termination was fully warranted. And Neal would later say that if Duane had evaluated me "it would have been in his role as a faculty member." The problem with that argument is that he was hired and paid as an administrator and as such taught very few courses, and none of the other part-time faculty evaluated full-time professors. I would also learn from the long-time Calvin HR director that in the late fall of 2002 Duane had asked her about the ramifications of terminating "someone who was a minority." She told me that she hadn't realized it was me but thought it to be a very curious question.

Behind-the-Scenes Story

Neal emailed me soon after Henry sent me his revised evaluation saying, "VP De Moor adjusted the body of his evaluation, but not his conclusion." This clearly raises another aspect of this "smoking gun." When Neal saw such a significant change relating to faculty evaluations in the second version, why didn't he question Henry regarding his original negative bias? It points to the fact that Neal was deeply involved from the very beginning, and that Duane had pushed the decision to fire me.

Most people get fired because they made the wrong person mad. If I made others at the seminary mad, I'm unaware of it. Not so, Duane. He was not officially in my chain of command, but I would find out quickly that un-officially he certainly was. I had sent an email to Neal in March, some nine months *before* I was terminated.

> I am writing about yesterday's meeting with you and Duane. . . I am very disheartened by what took place. . . . Let me emphasize that I got into this mess innocently. . . . My concern . . . prompted me to call Mary and ask if Duane had time to meet with me. She scheduled me in at 3 p.m. but Duane came to my office unannounced and asked to talk immediately. I asked the other person in my office to leave. . . . Duane's recollection of that time was that I was "monsterizing" him as though he were "stabbing the virgin Mary."

He was furious with me the moment he arrived. He did the talking, standing in front of my desk, towering over me. I wasn't about to get into a fight with him. But I did manage to interrupt his 20-minute harangue perhaps as many as a half dozen times—throwing my arms up and plaintively asking, *Why are you attacking me like this?*—thus, I presume, the "monsterizing" and "virgin Mary" accusations. I have no doubt he found my interruptions annoying.

The dust-up was not complex, and with faculty support, I managed to save the day. As a member of the chapel committee, I had earlier challenged Duane's decision to cancel on short notice a well-known speaker flying in from California. It was not because he didn't like the speaker, he insisted, rather because he wanted to take chapel in a different direction. I had no part in inviting this man to speak, but he had contacted me ahead of time and asked if we could meet while he was on campus. Because of my intervention, the speaker was not cancelled.

But because I had supposedly *monsterized* him, I was ordered to a meeting with him and Neal. I continue here with the email I sent to Neal the day after that meeting.

> I felt at the time and I feel now that Duane was seeking to intimidate me—so that I would never dare disagree with any of his policies again. I find that kind of mentality to be a very chilling one and one that flies in the face of any effort to not have us be a "dysfunctional" faculty—as seems to be an expressed goal. . . . I do not want to talk with Duane privately. I feel he has already misrepresented me terribly and I would want someone else present for any conversation we might have.

This "monsterizing meeting" (as I am identifying it) would take on a life of its own. Less than nine months later I was terminated. I had "made the wrong person mad."

Tell People You Wanted a Terminal Appointment

By mid-January, two weeks after I was fired, things were getting testy. Henry had caved in and given me the faculty evaluations, proving a very serious miscarriage of justice. I suspect Neal was looking for any possible way to cover up what had been done to me. By this time, the trustee board had rubber stamped the administration's proposal of putting me into a "renewal program." On January 14, very shortly after this, Neal sent me an email, among other things, writing:

> After thinking and praying . . . I urge you to take control of this program, including the very idea of doing it by making it your own. I urge you to tell people that your review has uncovered some deficits, that you are not satisfied with them, and that you are determined to address them. This way of proceeding preserves your dignity. . . . I have prayed for you every day. I have lost much sleep over your reappointment. . . . I repeat: own this program. Make it your own.

Once again, I was being shamed and demeaned in the name of prayer and preserving my dignity. Faculty members knew by this time that I was making appeals and fighting for my very academic life. Imagine telling them the whole thing was my "very idea." I showed Neal's letter to a colleague who wrote a very strongly worded letter, including the following paragraph.

I tell you in all candor that to now try and place the impetus for this recommendation on her and to add insult to injury as a way of "preserving her dignity" is something that I simply cannot fathom. . . . It is almost unforgivable for Christian administrators. Don't you realize that you are asking Ruth to lie—to herself and to the community—in order to have a remote chance of saving her job down the road. . . . [Y]ou cannot expect that Ruth will now be able to turn around and say in cheerful, cavalier fashion, 'well, you know I realized I had some deficiencies and I was not satisfied with myself and so I suggested a one-year terminal.' Sorry, that will not wash.

When I responded to Neal that I could not honestly do what he was asking of me, it only made the situation worse.

Judith and the "Smoking Guns"

Judith Bessant has written a detailed account of being fired from her faculty position at the Royal Melbourne Institute of Technology (RMIT). Her title: "'Smoking Guns': Reflections on Truth and Politics in the University." Though our worlds were far apart geographically and philosophically, we've had much in common. Like me, Judith took copious notes and assembled stacks of documents but, unlike me, she went to court and won. Her ordeal stretched out even longer than mine. "After nearly four years the matter ended up in the Federal Court which in May 2013 saw Justice Gray issue a damning judgment [and] order my immediate reinstatement and fine the university."

Like me and most women, Judith didn't step into her job in the manner male academics typically do: "In the late 1980s as a young academic . . . . with a crisp new PhD in hand, and a couple of infants in tow, I got my first academic job." She first found an entry-level teaching position but would soon become a professor at the prestigious RMIT. In 2017 she was awarded an "Order of Australia" for her noteworthy service, specifically her role as a social scientist. She has published some twenty books and many articles and has been recognized not only as an academic but also an advocate for young people at risk, particularly youth homelessness.

As I read her story, I felt for the first time that I had found a woman who had gone through what I had. Even while I was being harassed and hounded by the administrators, I continued to teach, sit on committees, lecture off campus, write books and articles—and serve as president of my professional organization. During those very same years, she was gaining recognition: "From mid-2004 I continued being an active researcher," she writes. "In that time, I was Chief Investigator on three large ARC grants, published five books, authored dozens of book chapters and many articles in refereed academic journals. I was formally identified as one of the top researchers within a very large school. I also carried a full teaching load." But too much success can be perilous for a woman.

In 2009, David Hayward became the dean and her immediate supervisor. Shortly thereafter he canceled her newly developed post-graduate program for which she had procured funds and prepared marketing promotions. She was blindsided. "This was done without consultation or prior notice," she writes. "He chose to communicate that information to me by email even though my office was adjacent to his." It was a major setback for her and for those who were planning to enter as graduate students. When David finally met with her, he did not disguise his hostility.

> This included making innuendoes referring to what he described as "historic events." Unbeknown to me at the time, those 'historic events' referred to my whistleblowing some 20 years earlier [for reporting a sexual assault]. Over the following months, and indeed years, I asked Professor Hayward for details. He refused, but continued with allusions to "those events."

The harassment continued and would take an emotional and physical toll on her health: "While I was on two weeks' leave recovering from [an] injury, my teaching was assigned to others," she writes. "Little did I know at the time, however, that plans had already been hatched by my Dean [David] and communicated to the VC [Dr. Margaret Gardner] who went along with his claim that it was a budget-cutting decision."

Justice Gray also found that "Professor Hayward harboured animosity" towards her. For that she endured "four hellish years." For me, three and a half. Studies have shown that women themselves, without realizing, discriminate against their own gender. In Judith's case, David reported to a woman. In fact, Justice Gray had some harsh words for this woman in court: "So you've got Professor Hayward [David]who has been gunning for Professor Bessant for some time," claiming it's about cost-cutting when it was not. "It's all a bit iffy." Yes iffy.

There had to be other reasons than cost-cutting. So, David would invent a new accusation in court—that she was "strongly anti-managerialist." It's a very interesting term in light of #17's wordy accusation of my being "excessively conformist to the predominant faculty ethos, especially when that ethos is negative"—in other words, "anti-managerialist."

David's accusation is laughable in that he was the one who initiated the charade. Instead of esteeming a faculty member for her awards and writing and teaching capabilities, he did everything he could to undermine and get her fired. Judith was accused of being anti-managerial, a code-word for pushy woman. Judith's situation screams sex discrimination, the very roadblock I encountered, which is detailed in the next chapter. In 2015, Elizabeth Broderick, Australia's Sex Discrimination Commissioner, articulated this very problem:

> Gender Equality is the unfinished business of the twentieth-first century. . . . So I will continue to use my voice to create an Australia that welcomes women, that cherishes their voice and eagerly awaits their wisdom. I will use my influence to create a world where a woman's value does not decrease because of another's inability to see her worth.

3

"Gender Tenured"

Sex Discrimination in Plain Sight

We know women are more likely to experience discrimination in the workplace than men. But the study shows the odds are higher still when women find themselves alone in a group of men. They are far more likely than others to have their judgment questioned than women working in a more balanced environment . . . [or] to be subjected to unprofessional and demeaning remarks.

Kevin Sneader and Lareina Yee,
"One is the Loneliest Number"

The most striking aspect of my teaching and subsequent termination from Calvin Seminary was that I was the first full-time female faculty member in the school's 125-year history and had continued to be the only one until my second terminal appointment had ended in 2006. It had occurred to none of my colleagues that the administrators would fire me. On one occasion the faculty-room discussion turned to attaining tenure and its touted job security. One of my colleagues turned to me in off-handed humor and said, *you have no worries; you're gender-tenured.* He was a friend and I laughed along with the rest. He meant no insult, simply that as a capable colleague and the only woman, I was as good as tenured. But he turned out to be dead wrong—wrong person, wrong gender. He was as shocked as anyone when I was terminated and removed from tenure track.

25

I certainly hadn't presumed I was more secure than my non-tenured male colleagues, nor did I imagine I would face blatant sex discrimination. But I did know I was an oddity. In fact, from the moment I was first contacted about filling an open position on the faculty, the process was carried out within an all-male Dutch Christian Reformed culture. Beginning with a small committee, then ministry division, full faculty, board, and synod, I ran the gauntlet and men determined the outcome. Those familiar with gender studies know that there are gender differences, for example, in the subject matter, wording and tone of questions men ask. I was aware of that, and it was what I had expected. I was also aware that many men who had weighed in on my appointment were opposed to hiring a female faculty member.

For some years, the CRC had been fighting a battle over women's ordination, and when I arrived the matter still had not been settled. In fact, had I been ordained, I would not have been eligible for a faculty position. But those who were not satisfied with my appointment were not men only. Many women who had fought for ordination were less than pleased. It would have furthered their cause had one of their own—a woman ordained in the CRC—become the first female professor.

Nevertheless, my hiring was viewed to be so groundbreaking that it made the front page of the *Grand Rapids Press*. For me, however, apart from the gauntlet, it was no big deal. I had previously been a lone woman on a faculty, albeit part-time, in a male seminary environment and I had assumed this would be no different. I can hold my own with the guys, sparring with them, taking a little ribbing and giving it back. And that was how I would describe my first two and a half years—until the heavy-handed administrators dropped the axe.

My initial support from colleagues quickly dissipated. Given a choice between the three insider administrators on the one hand and the lone woman outsider on the other, the least taxing on their schedules and their psychological wellbeing was obviously the former. Let the administrators handle the matter. My insistence that I wanted all the evidence scrutinized by them no doubt pushed them even further away. They were simply too busy to get involved. Added to that was my claim that this was sex discrimination. With that assertion, I had stepped over the line. I had been one of them in the faculty room. But with the use of one term, the atmosphere changed

Some colleagues actually chortled when I raised the issue of sex discrimination. How is sex discrimination even possible, they wondered aloud, when all three of the administrators had affirmed gender equality? They apparently assumed that the term is defined only by obvious statements followed by actions. If the administrators, for example, had said that a woman teaching at the seminary was "an abomination" (as a student had written in an evaluation) and then turned around and fired me, that would fit the definition.

Not the legal definition, however. If a woman who is as qualified as her male colleagues is singled out and terminated, that in itself is sex discrimination. I maintain that if my credentials had been placed alongside those of my colleagues (with name and gender masked), I would have ranked high. Thus, sex discrimination.

Systemic Sexism

Gender equality has made great cultural gains in the last few decades, but the administrators and my colleagues grew up with the notion of male superiority. The clergy were all men, as were elders, deacons, all those visible in a church service. The *ladies* were also important. They taught Sunday school and set the tables for church suppers. Such bias has not been magically eradicated. Today it's easily hidden behind the face of a woman or a man who outwardly affirms gender equality. I was accused by #17 of saying "very little in faculty meetings." But I can't even imagine the reaction there would have been if I, like one of my colleagues, had sometimes sounded off in a smug pontificating voice.

But none my colleagues would have recognized such gender bias or male privilege—with one notable exception. Though very conservative on political and social matters he was extremely well read and instinctively recognized the evil of injustice. He wrote to Neal and Henry some two weeks after that fateful night when Henry terminated me:

> Do you really want to be known as the ones who fired the first and only woman faculty member of Calvin Seminary? Ruth, recall, is not an unknown. Try to persuade a larger community that she is not good enough to crack the glass ceiling of male chauvinism in our institution.

Male chauvinism was plain as day in the seminary environment. How could the administrators and my colleagues have missed it? It was present in my classrooms every day, large framed pictures of white men looking down on me. They were the faces of all retired full-time faculty members since the founding of the school, men with rare exceptions who would not have countenanced a woman seminary professor. Positioned more than 8 feet high, one particular room often assigned for my classes had twenty-two of these portraits. Even larger portraits of the seminary presidents and administrators decorated the hallways.

But the chauvinism was not simply that of *dead white men*. Colleagues and board members evaluated me with bias. One colleague wrote: "She can generate some reactions that one might not expect (of a woman faculty)." What reactions might a *man* faculty be expected to generate? He didn't say. A board member, after he knew I had been given a terminal appointment, wrote: "I get the impression that Dr. Tucker loves to talk about and debate various issues. I found this challenging, but I wonder if some students might find this style a bit intimidating. . . . I hope she can take time to love her students (or perhaps take the time to show the love that is already there)." Students often stopped by my office to talk about personal matters because I did demonstrate a warm and caring approach in class. But the issue here is whether this man would have used these same words in evaluating a male professor? I seriously doubt it.

Later on, when the seminary board president agreed to put together an *ad hoc* committee to review my case, he asked me to write down the issues that should be mediated. I responded that the mediators should determine whether I was the most deficient professor on the faculty and whether the process was fair and honest—a very short and straightforward written statement. On reading that, another board officer accused me of being "melodramatic" in raising the issues. It was a blatant gender put-down. Women are deemed hysterical. They are out of control. They're melodramatic even when they ask straightforward questions—in a written memo, no less.

When I came to Calvin Seminary, I fully expected to encounter sex discrimination. How could it be otherwise—125 years of all-male administrators and full-time faculty? I took it in stride. Had I made an issue out of it, it certainly would have stymied my acceptance. I encountered gender jokes and teasing in the faculty lunch room, but I laughed along with the rest and took them in the spirit they were given. In fact, the guys didn't have to become choir boys just because I had joined them. I was determined to be *one of the boys*, a role that suited me and one that I thought would serve me best.

Dede Henley, however, has argued that one of the traps for professional women who are vastly outnumbered by men is "Being One of the Boys." The "tendency [is] to try to adapt and fit in to systems and rules built by men for men in the workplace." She goes on to say: "I challenge women leaders to change the way organizations and teams work." Excellent advice, but not for me. I was no leader. I was one lone woman at the bottom of the faculty totem pole. Bottom because I was, for the first year, the newest faculty member. As strange as it may sound, however, I felt fully their equal—until on that fateful night Henry terminated me.

Higher Demands on Me Than Colleagues

Henry's shocking decision revealed a standard no male colleague was required to meet. Never before was a colleague given a terminal appointment and removed from tenure track if two administrators (or even two colleagues) stated on a *faculty* evaluation that a professor should not be reappointed. Such is blatant sex discrimination. (In fact, in one instance an individual who was seeking an appointment for a teaching position had seven faculty votes against him. Yet he received the appointment. The administrators held power and they wanted him.

The Sex Discrimination Act of 1975 made it "unlawful for an individual to be discriminated against in the workplace in relation to selection for a job, training, promotion, work practice, dismissal or any other disadvantage such as sexual harassment." That Act was repeatedly violated during my time at the seminary. Also included is the following stipulation: "It does not matter what the employer's intention or motive was." A woman making a complaint needed "to make a comparison between how she was treated and how a man would have been treated. She can either point to an actual colleague, or refer hypothetically to how a man would have been treated." A colleague, challenging Neal and Henry, stated bluntly that the process was biased.

> I pointed out that the criteria of pedagogic excellence being applied [to her] were inappropriate for an initial reappointment since . . . none of the presently tenured faculty had ever been evaluated for their initial reappointment by these standards and that it was unjust to apply them to her. . . . [W]e are applying different, gender-biased criteria to her reappointment.

Within weeks after the fateful night with Henry, I was required to enter a "renewal program" and sign a "learning contract" if I was to have any chance of even fulfilling the one-year terminal appointment. The contract stated that on student evaluations I would have an average of 90% favorable ratings ("strongly agree" and "agree") in all categories, for example, "that teaching was engaging" or that "critical thinking was encouraged"—a standard no male faculty member had ever had to attain to have any hope of keeping his job. So here I was, under undue pressure with this requirement while trying to survive terrible workplace turmoil. But I was a good teacher. Indeed, before this contract was even fully formulated I exceeded that standard with 93% on my brand-new set of evaluations that had just been released. Neal would later commend me in a letter, saying that my student evaluations "rose to a fine level," though with no mention of colleagues not having a similar gun to their heads. More significant, that three-page letter devoted more than two pages to tearing me down—highlighting all that was wrong with me. The administrators had to carry on with their assault and *prove* I was deficient in order to counter questions faculty colleagues were asking.

Students and Sex Discrimination

If sexism were an issue among faculty and administrators, it is not surprising that the same would be true among the students. They also had grown up with all-male church leadership. One student had written: "A woman teaching at Calvin is an abomination to God." Another student commented on one of the final exam essay questions: "Lousy Pick—only a woman would quote this." My experience parallels the findings of statistical studies. In an "algorithmic sifting" of more than three million students who had participated on RateMyProffessors.com, Allison Bartlett asserts that words like brilliance and genius were far more often used of male professors than female. "So we know what's coming next," she continues: "As this is a gender mapping, women professors are consistently more likely to be described as feisty, bossy, aggressive, shrill, condescending, rude."

A significant majority of my students were male, and in some cases I had all-male classes. In most instances, students treated me with respect, and there were few times when I clearly noticed gender bias in the classroom setting. Studies have shown, however, that there is more discrimination against women faculty than is obviously seen. In one study, for example, students (male and female) were asked about the professor's promptness in grading and returning papers. The scores of the female instructors were 16% lower than their male counterparts—even though the papers had been returned at the same time.

When both male and female professors were teaching the same online course, the female was challenged about grades far more than the male professor. That was even when they switched their identities. The expectation is that she should go easier on students than a male professor. I find this particularly interesting because in the category of fairness in grading, students always evaluated me lower than in any other category.

I tried to be even-handed with my students, maybe to a fault. But at the same time, I was probably bringing up the rear in the *grade-inflation* marathon. When students complained that my grades were too low, I had assumed the problem was because I graded harder than my colleagues. I have come to doubt that assumption, convinced that I was perceived to be grading too hard because a woman is not supposed to be as tough as her male counterparts.

"A Kind of Contrariness"

Sex discrimination in everyday life is easily recognized by word usage. Indeed, anyone who has even an elementary understanding of gender issues, would recognize language that is demeaning to women. There are code words that raise red flags. Here is not the place to present a sexist language seminar, but I offer one illustration that points to the problem. The setting was a committee meeting of the 2005 Synod of the Christian Reformed Church. These are annual week-long gatherings, hundreds of delegates in attendance, meeting in plenary sessions and committees chaired by the directors of various denominational agencies.

As a seminary professor, I had been assigned to attend, serving as a faculty advisor for one of the committees. I sat unobtrusively in the back, some fifty in attendance, and listened to a number of reports that afforded afternoon nap time for some of the delegates. When there was an opportunity for questions, several delegates spoke up. Then during a lull, I asked for more specific details as a follow-up to a previous question. The chair's unsatisfactory response elicited more questions from delegates and stirred up some bickering. At one point a question was directed at me. I briefly offered my perspective which led to more questions and some charges of lack of transparency by the chair and his officers. It didn't occur to me that this interaction would be used against me by the administration.

I had simply asked a short well-reasoned question in a committee meeting. After the meeting adjourned, a number of people gathered around me asking if I could shed further light on the subject. I could not. Some were upset by the vague responses that were given by the director. This little *ruckus* was truly small potatoes. Anyone who has ever attended Synod knows that men do nearly all of the talking, sometimes long-winded monologues. They voice strong opinions and are sometimes embroiled in angry diatribes on the floor of Synod where the press and other outsiders can observe. My informal comments were made in a classroom with the doors closed.

But in that committee meeting was a man who would later write a letter to me, copying it to Neal. Although I did not know this man, he began the letter with simply "Ruth,". He referred to Neal twice as "Dr. Plantinga." This is a very common gender *faux pas*. Men are listed as "Dr." Women are listed as "Mrs." or by first name. This male writer then went on to say: "When I first met you I noticed a kind of contrariness." I had no recollection of ever meeting him at all, but that word simply screams sexism. (We all know *Mary, Mary, quite contrary.*) He went on to say: "you appear a little stand-offish and judgmental. . . . You came off making judgments. . . . You spoke in judgments, and with what came off as arrogance." You "reflected negatively . . . on the cause of women in leadership."

I cannot imagine a male professor receiving the same letter for doing precisely what I had done. Contrariness? Stand-offish, judgmental, arrogant, reflecting negatively on men in leadership? Really. But this man whom I did not know is not my focus. That he criticized me in a sexist and demeaning way is essentially beside the point. He was simply one synod delegate, with a Texas address on his letter. He had no doubt heard that I was challenging my termination, thus his copy to Neal.

What was disturbing, however, was that Neal did not even recognize the sexist language and disrespect. He was clueless, turning the letter around and using it as evidence against *me*. He never asked me about my interaction—or lack of it—with this delegate; he simply saved it as one more document to prove to mediators that I was too deficient to teach at the seminary. In actuality, however, it is a textbook example of sex discrimination. Here is the president of the institution, having terminated the only female full-time professor, turning a blind eye to blatant sexism. Is it any wonder that I would never be granted justice within the seminary confines?

Sheri Klouda and Sex Discrimination

Sheri Klouda, like me, was fired from a seminary. Her case, however, was fairly straightforward. There was no smoking gun or false reporting of student and faculty evaluations. Lies, yes, but apparently no shaming apart from the fact that she was female. Had she been male, she wouldn't have lost her job. Sheri had been hired as a biblical language professor in 2002 at Southwestern Baptist Theological Seminary in Fort Worth. This was one year before Meghan Lively was raped on that same campus. Both were wounded by the same man, none other than the seminary president, Paige Patterson.

Sheri had been teaching for only one year when Paige became president in 2003, the year he blamed Meghan for letting a young man inside her door, and then instructed her not to report her rape to law enforcement. Aware of his stance on women, Sheri was concerned about her own future. She requested an appointment with him and was relieved to learn that she "had nothing to worry about." Convinced her job was safe, she and her husband purchased a house.

The following year, however, Paige told her that she should look for a position elsewhere, this despite her teaching an over-load of courses and her excellent student evaluations. Her life was upended, not just professionally but financially as well. And she would be without family health insurance at a time when her husband was suffering from a serious heart condition. In the midst of threats and false promises, she managed to hold on to her job until the end of 2006.

Although Sheri was able to secure a teaching position at Taylor University in Indiana, she was stuck with a mortgage on a home that was very difficult to sell during an economic downturn. Her daughter was switching schools and leaving friends in the middle of a school year. "She's a young person and has her own opinions," Sheri commented. "She thinks it's unfair. She thinks it's wrong. She thinks this should have not happened. She thinks, 'They ruined my life too.'"

Two years later, March 20, 2008, a news item appeared from Fort Worth:

> A federal judge has ruled in favor of Southwestern Baptist Theological Seminary and its president, Paige Patterson, in a lawsuit by a former theology professor who claimed she was wrongly dismissed from a tenure-track position because she is a woman.

Sheri had filed the suit a year earlier. Judge John McBryde dismissed "all of her alleged actions against defendants" and ordered her "to cover the defendants' court costs." The wealthy Paige Patterson then made a statement: "My response is simply one of gratitude to God. . . . Americans everywhere may still rejoice in freedom of faith. . . . I am thankful to the thousands who prayed for us. I am thankful to the trustees. . . . I am thankful for our superb attorneys." Shameful god-talk. Sheri desperately needed funds to cover the cost of losing her position. In the end, she and her family were far deeper in debt.

Paige would get his just deserts but not until years later. After Megan and other women had testified about sexual assaults they had suffered in the churches and institutions of the Southern Baptist Convention, Paige would be one to lose his job. He was found guilty of very serious misconduct. A headline in *Christianity Today*, May 30, 2018 said it all: "Paige Patterson Fired by Southwestern, Stripped of Retirement Benefits." Two days later there was an update: "Paige Patterson lied to the board of [SWBT] about a rape allegation that came before him at another seminary, withheld documents from his previous presidency, and referenced attempting to 'break down' the victim of a more recent rape incident."

That summary statement barely touches the crimes of Paige Patterson. Sheri, a hard-working professor with good student evaluations, was crushed by a man who spoke often of God. God was on his side. He lied and slandered and sidelined an innocent professor and a young woman who was raped—crimes committed out of arrogance and contemptable self-righteousness.

Shadowy Sex Discrimination

Sheri Klouda was fired because Paige Patterson determined that, according to biblical precept, a woman could not teach Hebrew to male students. Such discriminatory beliefs and actions are hardwired among Southern Baptists and the broader evangelical community. Indeed, the list of what women cannot do seems to have grown longer every year, even as the dogma of female inferiority has hardened. Women are equal in *essence* to their male counterparts, the patriarchalists argue, but opportunities for ministry and leadership in the church and seminary are severely limited. So Sheri got caught up in a brutal and bald-faced scheme of sex discrimination. It was a straightforward story carried by a number of news outlets at the time.

My firing involved a much more shadowy form of sex discrimination. It was so deftly covered with layers of crazy quilts, making it indiscernible even by supportive colleagues—colleagues who could have, in fact, easily lifted the layers and discovered what lay beneath. But they were all men, and the only kind of sex discrimination, in their eyes, was equivalent to the blatant firing of Sheri simply because she was female. By that standard, the seminary administrators emphatically insisted my firing had nothing to do with gender. Rather, my case would shift to accusations of *ungodly conduct.* No gender specificity. But not so fast. As these charges were unraveled and exegeted it became very clear that I faced the worst kind of sex discrimination—charges so convoluted that insiders, much less news media, could not comprehend. It was as one colleague wrote in his evaluation, "the mysterious case of Prof. Tucker."

When the administrators' efforts failed to prove me a hopeless case as a colleague and teacher, they took a different tactic and charged me with *ungodly conduct* so serious that I was required to enter a "renewal program," as is detailed in chapter 4.

A recent decision by a federal appeals court [ruled] . . . that [Evangeline] Parker sufficiently alleged a hostile work environment based on sex, and it reinstated her claims. Noting that a male allegedly started the rumor and that those who allegedly spread the rumor were all male . . . that women, but not men, are susceptible to being labelled as "sluts" or worse.

Kathy R. Neal, "Sexual Rumors"

4

Slandered and Sidelined

Renewal for "Ungodly Conduct"

If accusations are not true, a person is in a situation similar to being bullied, [and] the psychological devastation can be ruinous. If you are not believed, if you cannot fight back with the true story, if now you are distrusted and under scrutiny, the sense of helplessness is overwhelming.

Dr. Carrie Barron, Psychology Today

I have no doubt that my situation was a clear case of bullying that resulted in feelings of helplessness on my part. The efforts to silence me with a *sealed environment* seemed at times overwhelming. There was no opportunity for me to defend myself against the charges leveled against me. I was slandered, silenced and sidelined.

A year earlier a colleague had been charged with plagiarism by a scholar from another institution. The incident occurred before the new three-man administration had taken over. An outside committee was immediately formed to review the case, and my colleague was given an opportunity to submit evidence, as was the scholar who made the charge.

As it turned out, this scholar had accused my colleague of stealing his interpretation of a biblical passage while the two of them were in conversation at a professional conference. Both were in the late stages of writing books, and when this scholar read the published volume my colleague had written, he cried foul. Whether or not conversation can be plagiarized did not actually become an issue because my colleague was able to prove with his own class notes as well as student notes that he had been teaching this new interpretation well before the conversation at the conference. The situation was handled professionally. My colleague was vindicated.

Indeed, plagiarism is a far more serious charge than low student or faculty evaluations. In the above case the male professor was treated fairly. As a woman I was discriminated against. I was summarily given a terminal appointment and removed from tenure track. I had no opportunity to have my situation judged fairly.

There was another incident of plagiarism at the seminary. A doctoral student was charged with plagiarizing the work of another student who had submitted his dissertation several years earlier. As a member of the disciplinary committee, I was directly involved. Initially this international student had claimed he did not understand American writing rules. But by the time he had appealed to our committee, his story had expanded. He told how he was typing his thesis on a hot day when a strong breeze blew through an open window. His own typed papers as well as those pages belonging to the other student got mixed up. Thus, he had inadvertently submitted large segments of the other student's work.

I think of that situation when I contemplate Henry's dishonest summation of my students' and colleagues' evaluations. He might have blamed a great wind that mixed up my evaluations with those of other professors. Had he been a student, however, his story would not have stood up to scrutiny. The student who appealed to the disciplinary committee was not allowed to graduate—a severe punishment. Henry carried on with no penalty whatsoever.

Truthfulness vs Dishonesty

Dishonesty was in plain sight in Henry's documents, soon to be followed by Neal's. The latter called me to his office less than two weeks after that fateful night with Henry. It was short notice and I had no advocate to accompany me. Also present was board president Sid Jansma. Neal opened by saying the purpose of the meeting was to talk about my renewal program. With no fanfare, he got right to the point. He asked me to tell my colleagues that I was the one who had come up with the idea of a renewal program.

I was taken aback, more than that, entirely flummoxed. Was he serious? To agree, as I wrote in my journal when I returned to my office "would have been an outrageous lie, but I was caught without a witness." I was confused and I acted the part. I feigned sluggishness, blaming sleepless nights on my "inability to understand what he was explaining to me." It was true that I'd been losing a lot of sleep and had a lot of anxiety. But was I really so terribly confused and muddled—utterly incapable of understanding what he was saying? So much so that he would have to explain it in a letter to me?

Call it a bald-faced lie if you will, but I prefer to think of it as *playing dead* when the enemy captain comes along and kicks my bloodied body. I understood exactly what he was saying. He was asking me to lie. I did lie. I said I could not understand.

Amid the sex discrimination at the seminary, occasional advantages emerged. I was consciously or unconsciously deemed lesser—a winey, anatomy-compromised, emotionally-fraught female, as old Aristotle used to say, "an incomplete male," or "as it were, a deformity." As such, I doubt any of my colleagues could have gotten by with feigning such confusion as to not understanding what Neal was saying. With tremors of a muddled mind, I asked if he could write to me what he was saying. I received the memo (previously mentioned) later that day, these words included:

> I urge you to take control of this program, including the very idea of doing it, by making it your own. I urge you to tell people that your review has uncovered some deficits. . . . [O]wn this program. Make it your own.

The following day, after I had made sure my upcoming sabbatical was secure, I wrote back in straightforward terms: "To . . . tell my colleagues that this one-year term of a supervised program is being done at my initiative would be untruthful." Shortly thereafter he accused me of "untruthfulness," claiming that in my letter I had said that he wanted me to "initiate" the program. That was a lie—presumably because "the very idea of doing it, by making it [my] own" was an "untruthful" way of saying "initiate." No doubt realizing, he was running out of accusatory options, he turned to what is defined as *slut-shaming*.

> "Slut-shaming" is the act of criticizing a woman for her real or perceived sexual promiscuity. Until now, much scholarship and journalism has focused on

the slut-shaming of school-aged girls and young women. This article [deals with] . . . slut-shaming in the American workplace.

Wendy N. Hess, "Slut-Shaming in the Workplace"

Slut-Shaming

In a small school, word quickly gets out if a faculty member is inadequate for the job, and my colleagues were not only bewildered but seriously questioning the accusations against me. Thus, the slut-shaming. My alleged *ungodliness* would power the rumor mill, having originated in a board meeting. Subsequently Neal sent me a memo with an accusation of unspecified "ungodly conduct." Colleagues advised me to make an appointment and demand an explanation, but I didn't trust him and wanted all communication to be in writing.

The slut-shaming continued until I left the school at the end of August in 2006. On one occasion, the previous president who had hired me, stopped by my office. When he had learned some two years earlier that I had been given a terminal appointment based on student and faculty evaluations, he was skeptical. So he asked me directly about my *ungodliness* the rumor mill was churning out. On November 8, 2004, I wrote the following in my CTS Journal.

> We talked for about 10 minutes and my situation came up. He asked again (as he has at least once before) if there was some scandal in my past with "that Holland doctor." When I emphasized that there was not and that I wanted all evidence and accusations, etc. to be put out on the table, he asked if there was scandal related to the Internet—heaven knows what he meant by that, maybe thinking that I was running a porn site.

CRC Defines Ungodly Conduct

People in the CRC know the meaning of the terms "ungodliness" and "ungodly conduct." In fact, I mentioned the accusation to the former academic dean—a fair-minded man who had strongly supported me in my teaching before he left to take another position. If it were *ungodliness*, he said, you would have been out of there in a heartbeat. Exactly.

The CRC *Manual for Synodical Deputies* clearly defines the term with the following example: "Reinstatement to office shall be denied to individuals who . . . confessed to or are determined to be guilty of sexual misconduct and other related ungodly conduct." If the reader still does not know what "ungodly conduct" means, the manual explains: "Examples of related ungodly conduct include, but are not limited to, participation in pornography, engaging in sexual contact in return for payment or any other favor, or voyeuristic behavior, displays of sexually offensive material, suggestive gestures and remarks, and other sexually intimidating behavior."

In short, only weeks after I had been terminated, I was slut-shamed to cover up for Henry's dishonest summaries of my student and faculty evaluations. I am not alone. A study in 2011 found that nearly half of American women have been slut-shamed. "In its purest form," writes J. R. Thorpe, "slut-shaming is an attack on someone's character and reputation."

I had first learned that the term ungodliness was used against me when Neal spoke of it in a board meeting less than two weeks after that fateful night. I was leaving campus, having been asked nearly a year earlier to deliver the second-term convocation lectures at Dordt University in Iowa. A colleague, at my request, had been given an opportunity to briefly defend me. When he was finished, he was asked to leave the room. He returned, however, only minutes later to grab his briefcase. That is when he heard Neal's reference to "ungodliness."

When I returned to the seminary after my lectures in Iowa, I learned that the board had decreed that I should be placed in a "Renewal Program." If I had been an incompetent teacher or colleague, I wouldn't have needed *renewal*, rather pedagogical help. *Renewal* is apparently reserved for a slut. No such program had ever been fashioned at Calvin Seminary before, and I immediately recognized it as an effort to further shame me. Indeed, my *renewal* was anything but confidential. It was scheduled to be announced at the next faculty meeting—as it actually was. I was present when all my colleagues were asked to pray for me as I entered this renewal program. And that was supposed to "preserve my dignity?"

Renewal Program for a Woman Only

This was a program designed for the only woman at the seminary. And thus, there was no blueprint and there were no women available to "renew" me. But finding men was not a piece of cake either. Initially three of my tenured colleagues were selected. For various reasons, they wisely got out of it. They then asked a retired colleague with whom I had worked closely, but he realized quickly it was a set-up to further humiliate me. He declined. Things dragged on, and then in mid-February a female board officer requested that a "facilitator" be brought in to help make resolution. She named a psychologist who was in private practice, a woman who was a mediator well-known in CRC circles (though I had never heard of her). That didn't fly with the administrators, and no wonder

In March of 2003, I had sought support from colleagues (as I had been doing all along)—trying to persuade them to call for an outside committee as had been done with our colleague charged with plagiarism. On April 2, 2003, I received an email from Henry stating: "What I am hearing from some colleagues and what I heard about the most recent faculty meeting [at which he was absent], I am beginning to think that you are still in the mode of protesting what you consider to be an unfair decision. . . . You have a choice. Carry on with this 'battle' or enter a program of renewal in good faith." I understood that I had only one option. I responded with one sentence: "I will enter a program of renewal in good faith." Though seething on the inside, I was too timid to bring up his own egregious bad faith. After that board member Jack Nyenhuis and retired professor Mel Hugen agreed to take on the task of further humiliating me. Our first session was May 2, 2003, exactly four months after that fateful late January afternoon with Henry. Apparently not wanting to deal with my alleged "ungodly conduct," their first action was to change the name to Faculty Development Program. Their guide would be a letter to me from Neal in late January identifying nine of my "deficits" and "lapses." One related to a new online teaching program. Faculty had widely complained that we had not been properly trained. I actually had figured things out better than most, but, of course, I was the one cited for deficiencies. Neither Jack not Mel knew anything about online teaching. A similar accusation related to my teaching in the M.A. program.

Some of his charges were oddly short and vague. Neal had simply written: "Give others the benefit of the doubt"—as if it were a universal Christian principle. Another fuzzy charge was simply: "Take a constructive role in meetings." He offered no evidence that I had not done that. Still another: "Gain a reputation for Godliness." I have to assume that directive was intended to reverse his accusation of my "ungodliness." I responded at some length to these nine charges, but Neal had wanted acknowledgments and apologies.

These charges (minus my response) would become the unchallenged foundation for this renewal program. I had asked these two men if they had seen any of the documents related to my termination. Both said they had not. I asked if they would look at them. They refused. Instead, they accepted Neal's *commandments* (ten minus one) as though, coming down from Mount Sinai on slabs of stone, they were the very words from God on high.

I found this first meeting (and the ones that followed) to be demeaning. When it was over, I wrote to a friend and colleague from another school:

> I just came out of my first 'renewal' meeting with Mel and Jack. I knew full well that they are "hired" by the other side and they're not remotely what might be termed mediators. But they both emphasized that they were there because I chose them (which I didn't) to be there to help me, the implication being that I should be very grateful for their services. This is all part of the authoritarian power play that is going on.

Crying Shame of a Learning Contract

Mel and Jack carried out their duties for the next few weeks, piling on more shame. My duty was to formulate a "learning contract." I took it very seriously because I knew it was the only way out of the program. Though I had never heard of the term before, I assumed I could focus on my teaching rather than on my alleged ungodly conduct (which was not even broached). I googled:

> A learning contract is a voluntary, student-completed document that outlines actions the learner promises to take in a course to achieve academic success. This contract is signed by the student, the instructor, and (optionally) the parent.

When I presented a written copy to Jack and Mel they spent a few minutes looking it over. Mel was the first to speak. He disparaged it, insisting it was so bad that he could not recommend my continuing at the school. I was stunned. I could not speak. I simply wept. Then Jack spoke, saying that I had actually included everything they had asked for, but it was not in proper outline form. He suggested how to turn my short paragraphs into outline form as I nodded and took notes. He asked me if I had any questions. I shook my head. He asked me if I could attach a copy of my revised learning contract to an email that afternoon. I nodded. He asked me if I would close in prayer. Still stifling sobs, I shook my head. He prayed and the meeting ended.

I'll never forget that day as long as I live: Mel's cruelty, my weeping, and Jack asking me to pray. It was May 15. I had arrived at school early, as I always did. And then that phone call. North Carolina. She identified herself. Church secretary. I had recently visited the church and met her. I knew immediately. My dear friend Alan Neely had died. He had been very ill, and the news was not unexpected. Then the phone call from Bill O'Brien. We had been best buddies at professional meetings, Alan a professor at Princeton Theological Seminary, Bill at Beeson Divinity School. Bill and I cried and reminisced for a half hour. We had both visited the Neely home recently and we recalled the many good times the three of us had enjoyed together.

As we said our goodbyes, I looked at the clock. It was time for my meeting with Mel and Jack. I rushed to the restroom and washed my face in cold water, toweled off and put on makeup. Both were seated as I entered the room desperately trying not to give a hint that anything was wrong. It never occurred to me to share with them my great sorrow. They were there to demean me—nothing else. Later that day I would submit the very same "learning contract" I had submitted early that morning, though in outline form. Both signed off on it. If, apart from his asking me to pray, the reader might think Jack was fair-minded, but there is more to come. As to Mel, I do not recall encountering him again after that meeting.

Janay Garrick and Moody Bible Institute

When I first read Janay Garrick's account of being fired, I recognized the parallels with my own story. I almost wondered if administrators at Moody Bible Institute (MBI) had read "My Calvin Seminary Story" blog. If Calvin could falsify summaries of evaluations and get away with it, why couldn't they? If Calvin could move the goal posts on why I was being fired, why couldn't Moody? If Calvin could get by with blatant sex discrimination, why not MBI? Maybe male administrators don't need a playbook; perhaps such treatment of a woman comes naturally. Like me, Janay was not fired because she did something wrong; she was fired because she made someone mad.

Moody administrators, like those at Calvin Seminary, would falsify Janay's student and faculty evaluations and then, when she demanded the documents be opened up, they moved the goal posts and brought up new charges.

> [S]tudent evaluations of my classroom performance landed me squarely in the "Meets Expectations" to "Exceeds Expectations" to "Outstanding" categories.' Moody administration had rated me "Below" [and] "Barely Meets Expectations" in Teaching Performance.

The administrators also claimed she had low peer reviews, which were mysteriously unavailable when she asked to see them. Equally mysterious was the fact that she had never been asked to write peer reviews of her colleagues. Later at her performance review, Janay refused to sign their document agreeing with their assessment of her.

With no measurable evidence to continue, the "administration switched tactics for my termination," she writes, "suddenly claiming that I could not sign the doctrinal statement because I was egalitarian," believing that "women should **not be excluded** from any role, function, or office within any sphere—work, church, home." She had hidden nothing when she was hired in 2014, including the fact that she was an ordained minister. But she was a rising star in her field, and they wanted her genius at Moody.

So, why was she fired? No real mystery, it's not rocket science. A female student had approached her in 2016, having been barred from changing her major to pastoral ministry, a major for boys only. That would have been perfectly legal before 2011. But in 2012 Moody had begun receiving Title IX money—financial aid for students from the federal government. This wasn't small potatoes—the amount exceeding $24 million. Required to meet federal terms and conditions, Moody officials hid from regulators their lack of compliance, that is until Janay outed them. It was a grueling procedure, but at the end of the day, the student (and Janay) had won—though Moody would continue for more than a year to drag its feet.

Like me, Janay would not bow out easily. And as was true in my case, the administrators wanted everything done internally and confidentially. "They railroaded me in the grievance procedure," she writes, "doing everything in their power to ensure that I could not possibly receive a fair 'hearing' of my peers." They would not allow evidence relating to their falsified student evaluations. And worse yet, the very dean who had fired her became the school's arbiter and prosecutor even though, as she rightfully claimed, he was a "hostile witness." She concluded that the school was "not searching for justice, but in fact and in deed, obstructing justice!" All of this would be another area of common ground I had with Janay. Why would either one of us have imagined we might find justice through internal channels?

Unlike me, Janay went to court. She lost. The attorneys for Moody argued that the judge should dismiss her claims because she could not comply with the school's religious doctrines. It was unconstitutional, they argued, for the federal government to interfere with their freedom of religion. The judge agreed, apparently paying no attention that her "religious doctrines" hadn't changed since she was hired.

According to an online report (October 13, 2020), however Moody was not yet off the hook. The headline makes that clear: "Bible College Must Face Sex Discrimination, Retaliation Lawsuit." Moody was represented by Bryan Cave Leighton Paisner LLP, with offices not only in Chicago but also in many other American cities and offices as far away as London, Dubai, Hong Kong and Moscow. Janay, since having moved to Moscow, Idaho, was representing herself. True, the court had no oversight on religious doctrine, which Moody had claimed was the issue. But Janay rightly pointed out that doctrine was simply a ruse for sex discrimination and retaliation against her for helping a student file a Title IX claim.

Slandering with a Sealed Environment

The administrators at Calvin Seminary did not seal their *own* environment. They leaked and talked and sent out memos and made public announcements, while they demanded I operate under strict rules of *confidentiality*. They knew how to control the environment. The terms they used were devastating to my case. After I caught Henry in serious dishonesty, they began their propaganda machine with a vocabulary that would ruin any hope for justice.

Janay sums up her situation that so closely parallels my own.

[M]en at every level of leadership—from faculty to administration—lied *to* me and *about* me (about my hiring process, about my job performance, about the circumstances surrounding my firing). They lied openly and unashamedly to my students. [They] practiced obfuscation, clever semantic tricks, double-talk and word play to cover up the gender discrimination. . . . Then, they colluded to fire me first through a falsified negative performance evaluation, and then, when they couldn't make that "stick," they suddenly claimed that I could not sign the institution's doctrinal statement.

Janay's words are all mine. When Neal spoke publicly that he was seeking to *preserve my dignity* he was actually doing the very opposite. He demanded renewal for ungodly conduct, for lapses, for deficits, for deficiencies, for ungodliness. Colleagues had not believed I had gotten low student and faculty evaluations. But many believed Neal sincerely wanted to preserve my dignity. Only a very serious transgression, they reasoned, would merit a terminal appointment and removal from tenure track. Sidelined from my colleagues, I was lonely and vulnerable.

I felt insecure and fragile. I felt the sting of humiliation in every session with Jack and Mel. I felt a lack of self-control, sobbing when Jack disparaged me. Of course, I was grieving Alan's death. It was a severe loss. But was it more than that? Why wasn't I able to man-up and hold my own in the presence of two pathetic men? Was there something else going on? Was it hormones? Was it menopause? Was it hot-flashes? Was it because of dizziness, because of fatigue? These gender differences shape Chapter 5.

> The psychological symptoms associated with the menopause such as loss of self-confidence, low self-esteem, anxiety and depressive symptoms are the ones that often affect women the most.
>
> Louise R. Newson, "Menopause Discrimination is a Real Thing"

5

Hot Flashes and Hardball

Gender Differences Disregarded

The best thing I find is a . . . little ice-pack thingy . . . about the size of a Big Mac . . . that I can "discreetly slip it into my bra" when I feel a hot flash coming on. . . . I'm trying to picture exactly how I would go about discreetly slipping [it] into my bra at a faculty meeting without anyone noticing.

Jennie Young, "Let's Put 'Hot' in Hot Flashes"

The last class I taught at the seminary was on leadership, the content drawn largely from a volume I was contracted to write. One of my sessions related to gender and leadership styles. It was a small class, only about a dozen, one woman. I began one session by asking the students how the seminary might be different if it had been founded by women and only women had served as administrators and faculty. By now students would have known I had been terminated and easily recognized I was reversing my own situation. I had hoped my question would stimulate discussion. It didn't. Silence hung heavy in the air swallowed by large portraits on the walls of twenty-two white men.

Before I was fired I might have thrown the question out for faculty lunch discussion. I can hear the jokes and laughter and guffaws. And I would have laughed along. It's what a woman has to do. But there's a very serious side to my question as well. I had been studying gender issues for

49

decades. I had shelves of books on the topic, one of which was Deborah Tannen's *You Just Don't Understand* (some four years on the *New York Times* bestseller list). I doubt the administrators or my colleagues had ever heard of her. Except for one, there simply was no indication that they might have read anything by this renowned linguist, a PhD from UC Berkeley, professor at both Princeton and Georgetown Universities. Katy Kelly writes:

> Deborah Tannen—who has spent much of her career studying the verbal war between the sexes—thinks she has at least part of the answer. An expert in linguistics, Tannen, 45, has spent 17 years recording and analyzing other people's conversations. As she explains in her fifth book, *You Just Don't Understand—Women and Men in Conversation*, many of the problems . . . . stem from the basic differences in how each sex uses language.

Women and "Troubles-Talk"

Tannen later cleared up a misconception about the book—a misconception she had inadvertently brought on herself. Her studies had shown that women, far more than men, engage in "troubles talk," while men, as soon as a woman begins talking about troubles, offer a fix. Women are the yakkers. Men are fixers. In responding to that issue, she conceded that women want to tell their stories, but they also want solutions. Before a solution can be discussed, however, a woman wants a man to ask questions: What happened? What did you say? How did he respond? Good advise comes only after the issues are understood.

Almost all of my colleagues, to a man, had advice to give—solutions to get me out of the mess I was in. Four of them said right off the bat, *I'd get a lawyer if I were you.* Perhaps good advice. But no one asked first what kind of nest egg I had in order to afford such a lawyer. Not one asked me if I knew attorneys around town who had never represented the seminary or college (ones I would learn quickly would turn me away). And not one said he knew an attorney who could give me free advice before I began paying him $300/hour.

My colleagues had snappy advice, but they did not want to get involved. They did not want to hear my story and to look at my documents. Every one of them, to a man. But for one. Yes, I admit I wanted "troubles-talk" from them. But even the term screams sexism. What about a man who can actually afford to go to a high-priced attorney? Does he engage in "troubles-talk"? Does the attorney actually listen to his story? Does the attorney ask questions? Does *he* offer advice on how together they can fix the trouble? Of course, even if it is a male attorney, that is the way it is done. Men do engage in "troubles-talk" when they are in trouble.

Not to say there is no gender difference here. Yes, women generally do not want an immediate fix, and men more often do. But neither the administrators nor my colleagues recognized these gender differences. They did not understand that I, perhaps more than other faculty members, needed to talk things out. If they had read the literature and cared, they would have known about such gender differences.

A Menopausal Professor and More

Most of my students had no choice but to recognize me as though I were a different species from the rest of their professors. I *was* different. Physical features, of course. But unlike my colleagues, I endured irregular monthly cycles that would often trigger hormonal upheavals. Some women may be able to hide a hot-flash while standing in front of a class. Not me. I would suddenly become overheated, my face turning red as I gripped the podium. It might happen two or three times during a class or not at all. I quickly learned to take them in stride and carry on. I had borrowed a toy from my little granddaughter—a hand-held, bright-colored, battery-operated cylinder with a duck on top. Press the button and the duck would rapidly flap its wings. I would have preferred standing in front of an air-conditioner, but the flapping wings actually helped—and it alerted my students to the fact that *Mama* was having a hot flash.

Sometimes I would need to walk to the back of the room and open a window for fresh air, but I always managed to keep things going without noticeably disrupting the class. In fact, some of the more talkative students recognized this as the perfect opportunity to jump in and take over. With my colleagues, however, it was different. Before that fateful night when Henry fired me, I enjoyed faculty-room fun and debate. We laughed and joked and discussed virtually any subject that came up. Never menopause, however. "It's no surprise that the impact of menopause in the workplace isn't much discussed," writes Anne Loehr. "Most organizational systems were built by and for men, rarely with women in mind, let alone women with menopausal symptoms. So there's an inherent sexism and bias built into organizations."

After I had been terminated, however, when I no longer felt safe in the faculty room, the issue did arise. It was during a formal faculty meeting. Faculty sat around tables arranged in a U-shape, the three administrators seated at the top of the U. I always sat on the side nearest the door to get out—for obvious reasons. On one occasion I had slipped out of my seat, walked through the open space that led to the door, pulled a chair next to a window, opened it and hung my head out. The men were disputing some issue and I had assumed I was hardly noticed. I could hear the debate and the fresh air was cooling me off. I was about ready to get up, walk back, and slip into my chair when Neal broke into the discussion. *Are you okay, Ruth? Is something wrong?* I said: *I'm just having a hot flash.* There was silence. Dead silence. I walked back to my chair. Colleagues were shuffling papers. No one made eye contact, but for one colleague who had openly supported me. His elbows on the table, hands folded over his mouth, his eyes merry.

Never did the administrators—or male faculty and staff, for that matter—ask me how things were going as the only full-time female on the faculty. It apparently never occurred to them that women's issues are different from men's. And they didn't want to know. In fact, the onset of menopause for me began late, around age fifty-five when I started teaching at the seminary. It began with very heavy periods sometimes necessitating various sanitary products in multiples—a most unfortunate condition when teaching long afternoon classes. I lost so much blood that I was often dizzy and fatigued and I would need two D&Cs. On one occasion, I had to wait days to see a doctor. He ordered two units of blood before he would release me. I'll never forget how spirited I was as I parked my car and walked through the halls to get my mail. How I loved those units of blood.

Had there been women on the faculty and in the administration, things would have been very different. "I want all my sisters to join me," writes Anne Loehr. "Let's make some noise about this hot flash thing. Let's normalize it like carpal tunnel or restless leg syndrome. If we're effective, we could *at least* lobby for legally mandated hot flash breaks."

Humor aside, a Harvard Med School website has taken menopause very seriously. "The outward signs of a hot flash — sweating and pink or reddened skin — tell the world that a woman's estrogen production is dwindling." Tell the world—or maybe only two dozen students in a seminary classroom. "Heart palpitations and feelings of anxiety, tension, or a sense of dread also . . . complain[ts] of burning up . . . chills . . . night sweats . . . fatigue and mood changes. . . ."

I experienced all those symptoms and more: "Some women report that they perspire so profusely that they soak the bed linens and wake up." I recall dozens of times during those early years at the seminary when I would wake up in a wet bed, head to toe, chilled to the core. "The problem is a troublesome one that can leave sleep-deprived women fatigued, tense, irritable, and moody." Did my colleagues suspect that I might be enduring these physical and emotional difficulties? I doubt it. For more than a century the school had been a clueless all-boys club.

"There's No Crying in Baseball"

The film "A League of their Own" (1992), directed by Penny Marshall, starred Tom Hanks, Geena Davis, Madonna—and Bitty Schram. When Hanks, the manager of the all-woman team, screams at Bitty for an unforced error she starts crying. He's absolutely incredulous. What on earth is she doing? Then his cynical words, "There's no crying in baseball." It's a very funny episode, and his words have stood the test of time.

I played ball on a church league and never once cried. I did cry during a renewal session, however, and I got "written up" for it. Why wouldn't Jack have just looked incredulous and said, "There's no crying at seminary." And there was no crying across the street at the college either, at least there wasn't supposed to be. I had spoken with a female professor fighting a tenure matter and noted in my Journal: "The other thing I have in common with [her] is our frustration with crying on occasion. She said she cried the other day when meeting with her dean."

"Many women in the workplace go to great lengths to avoid crying in front of coworkers," writes Melody Wilding. "From slinking off to the bathroom to internally telling themselves to 'buck up' there's a sense that crying in a professional setting is just about the *worst* thing you can do." Yes, the *worst thing you can do*. I sobbed in my "renewal program" with Jack and Mel.

Two years later, when I was finally getting support to form an *ad hoc* committee of the Board of Trustees to review my case, Jack was part of the discussion. When board president Sid named Jack to chair this committee, I objected. Documents had shown that he had been involved in my situation and supported Neal even before that fateful night with Henry. And he had admitted in our first *renewal* meeting that he had never actually seen material related to my case.

In light of this, I stated that he should recuse himself. Jack insisted he could be fair. And here's the kicker. He actually said this: *I've never told anyone about the time you cried during our meeting.* So, the proof that Jack could be fair was that he never blabbed around that I was a weepy woman—though he was telling those in the room that very moment. Crying is indeed, *the worst thing* a woman in the workplace can do.

And Jack would chair the *ad hoc* committee.

A situation very similar to mine is told by Melody Wilding on *Forbes Women*. Her client was having a very bad day, as I was when I had learned of Alan's death just before that meeting with Jack and Mel.

> My client, Elizabeth, recently told me a story about how she crumbled during a tense discussion with her boss. She had worked hard and long on her latest project and was expecting a glowing response. When they met, Elizabeth was already having a horrible day, and when her boss gave a more critical reaction than expected, Elizabeth felt herself tearing up. She didn't have time to "escape" somewhere to cry privately, and she ended up crying in the meeting.

Women Letting Men Save Face

If women do well in "troubles talk" and crying in baseball, they also do well in letting men *save face*. In 2003, less than two weeks after my teaching career was torpedoed, I was asked out to dinner by a professional couple, she a college administrator, he a CEO of a mid-size company. She emphasized process and how I needed to focus on the administrators' utterly failed process. He jumped in by stressing that I had to let the administrators save face. You've got to let them have a way out by which you can let them save face. I did that. In fact, I look back on my earliest responses, and I'm giving away the store, while several of my colleagues are telling me that they would get a lawyer if they were in my situation.

An article by Padraig O'Morain in *The Irish Times* (3-18-08), is titled, "Help someone save face and preserve dignity." It caught my eye immediately, because in their repeated shaming of me, the administrators' stated goal—written and oral—was always to "preserve her dignity." Padraig begins the article with reference to his own gender:

> **THAT'S MEN:** Losing face in public is the most devastating, leaving you with a terrible sense of shame. . . . You are at work and you make a mistake.

Your boss is a bit of a bully. . . . Because you have lost face in front of colleagues . . . you find it hard to look them in the eye.

It is interesting that my friend, the CEO, was far more concerned about saving the face of the administrators than saving my face. But he was, after all, trying very hard to save my job. And he certainly knew that if I were to gain ground the administrators would need to save face—to save their collective face after their shocking shaming of me.

Playing Hardball with a Puffball

On January 5, 2003, three days after that fateful evening with Henry, I wrote to him about how I was being treated differently from my colleagues. I cited an article by a woman who was the first female faculty member in a department at a secular university. She told about her experience as well as those of other women. Included in my letter was the following paragraph:

> What I remember most about the article was a statement that summed up their collective experiences. The statement was that women are expected to play 'hard ball' with the men on the faculty, which the author was not necessarily objecting to. The only problem is that women are expected to play 'hard ball' with a 'puff ball.' This is how I sometimes feel at CTS. . . . The message I sometimes seem to get from the current administration (and on some of the faculty evaluations) is that, if I play ball at all, it better be with a 'puff ball.' There is not a level playing field for women on the CTS faculty.

This letter was copied to Neal, but neither he nor Henry responded. I have to smile when I read this paragraph now some two decades later. With all its qualifiers it's an example of "puff-ball" language: I *sometimes* feel . . . *some* on the faculty. . . . I *sometimes seem* to get. . . ."

I do believe the administrators expected me to play hardball with a puffball. I suppose I could have made the change, but playing puffball in the faculty room was not natural for me, so after I was fired I simply stayed away. But I would repeatedly respond in puffball language to the administrators because that was the only way I could keep my job. When I was forthright, as when I laid out my credentials requesting reappointment ten months after I was fired, Henry accused me of having "boxing gloves on."

Women and the "Double Bind"

Some women simply are not cut out to play hardball. In their book *Hardball for Women*, Pat Heim and Tammy Hughes tell about Lara, a Silicon Valley engineer who was the only woman on a team. The team met often in consultation with each other, and Lara felt she was holding her own—that is until her male supervisor dressed her down: "I want you to stop talking at my meetings altogether. You're slowing down progress for all of us by asking questions and trying to talk through things too much." With two children to support on her salary alone, she kept quiet, not daring to risk her job.

> It was even more painful to her that none of the male peers on her team seemed to miss her voice or even try to draw her into their discussions. Lara had become a noncontributor, and that's a loss not only for her personally but also for her team and company. If men can be brought to understand the tension of the double bind for women ("be a woman but act like a man—but not too much, or you'll be judged a bitch"), we can all manage female advancement better.

While reading literature on the differences between male and female in the workplace, the term *double bind* often arises. The workplace standard is typically based on a masculine way of doing things. Women are expected to adjust. In "Stanford Finds 'the Secret Switch For Women's Success!,'" Caroline Turner writes: "Women are perceived as too soft or too tough but never just right." So what is Stanford's "secret switch"? Essentially, a woman must be both masculine and feminine: She will do well if she "can turn these traits on and off." She must be very keen on when to do this, "depending on the circumstance." Had I been fired for not always doing the *switch* at the right time, I plead guilty.

Regarding faculty meetings, a staff member (#7), one of two who voted against my reappointment, wrote that I was "reactive and combative in faculty meetings." The other administrator who voted against my reappointment (#17), however, wrote: "She says little in faculty meetings. I often find Ruth to be excessively conformist to the predominant faculty ethos. . . ." Scholars who have researched the "double bind" might say that this lone woman on the faculty was new and *excessively conformist*, perhaps *combative*, trying too hard to be *one of the boys*. Colleague #14, however, summed up my role in faculty meetings: "Quiet but steady."

Sexism, Racism and the Firing of Denise Isom

I was not just the lone woman, but a single lone woman with married male colleagues. And I was lonely. Imagine, however, a black single woman on the nearly all-white faculty of Calvin College (now university). She was Denise Isom. The school was proud of its diversity, always seen in promotional publications. Students are sitting on the lawn and walking together to a classroom—always a student of color among them. Even as there was supposedly no sex discrimination at the seminary, there was no race discrimination at the college. Or was there?

"Calvin College's board," writes Sarah Zylstra in *Christianity Today*, "has denied the request of an African American professor to worship at her . . . African American congregation, Messiah Missionary Baptist church." If she refused to quit her church, Denise Isom "will be taken off tenure track and given a one-year term." There were plenty of white churches she could have attended and some multi-cultural ones that she had visited, but none felt right: . "I need a place of worship that is already consistent with my culture and able to grapple with issues of race in ways which make it a respite, a re-charging and growing place for me, as opposed to another location where I must 'work' and where I am 'other.'"

Provost Claudia Beversluis—with her nice Dutch name—weighed in: "I wish there were a [Christian Reformed] congregation in Grand Rapids that was fully multicultural or even that there was one that was largely African American." She gave Denise two options. Those included her giving up her teaching position or going to a largely white church. I weighed in as well—in a letter to the editor (11-5-07), responding to an article that appeared in the *Grand Rapids Press*:

> It was sad to read about Calvin College not permitting Denise Isom to find her church family with Messiah Missionary Baptist Church, a landmark faith community in Grand Rapids. . . . As a Calvin faculty member, she is required to join a church with the "right" Reformed theology, with no consideration for where she might find fellowship most conducive for worshipping God. Her options? She can attend a white, mostly Dutch-American church or one of the very rare Reformed multi-cultural churches in town. But Caucasian faculty are not forced into these limited options such as an African-American or multi-cultural church. The Calvin community just doesn't get it, as I discovered when I, as the only woman faculty member (and an outsider), was hounded out of the Seminary. They just don't get it.

I don't pretend to understand the issues Denise was expressing. Having lived for nearly three decades in a mostly black neighborhood, however, and having worked beside a black business partner, I do know that there are far more than surface differences between how the races do church. For many, the black church experience is as deep as race itself—as deep as gender.

"You've Just Got to Suck It Up"

Get over yourself. "You've just got to suck it up." The very words of one of my male colleagues. Perhaps Denise heard those words as well. She left the college and was offered a position at California Polytechnic State University. I left the seminary when my second terminal appointment expired and was unable to secure another full-time position. In both cases it was a loss for John Calvin's schools. Both institutions insisted there was neither race or sex discrimination, and in both instances the administrators just *didn't get it.*

The differences between male and female should not have been rocket science for the seminary administrators or my colleagues. The literature was everywhere. In fact, the book of the quarter (a custom initiated by Neal) chosen for the spring of 2005 was Gender and Competition: How Men and Women Approach Work and Play Differently by Kathleen De Boer. The book presents many stories of gender differences. Coaches like film star, Tom Hanks, can berate their male players who typically go back on the floor or out to the field and play their hardest. But women simply don't function that way amid hostility and abuse. To get back on the playing field and functioning again, they need to talk things out and make necessary apologies.

Had the three administrators even read this book of the quarter? Had my faculty colleagues? Or would they first learn of this example only when I was permitted to speak before them in November of 2005? After giving the above example, I went on to say:

> One of . . . my colleagues said to me, "You've just got to suck it up." *Forget what they did to you . . . come back to the faculty room and have a good time like you used to.* But I find it very stressful and difficult to function in a situation when there is unresolved hostility and alienation. . . . To pretend that everything is fine, without talking it out, is something I'm not capable of doing.

For much of my time at Calvin Seminary, I was going through what is euphemistically called *the change*. Menopause seemed never to end. But many women have found this season of their lives liberating—as I might have—were I not being callously fired at the same time. In "The Secret Power of Menopause" (*The Atlantic,* October 2019), Liza Munda writes: "To describe [this] passage of life, even a painful one, can itself be a form of empowerment." Writing my description has truly been empowering—and hopefully a teaching opportunity to male administrators. Had the seminary administrators been women, matters would have progressed entirely differently. But of course, they were men. I said nothing about menopause and they didn't ask. But they did pay extra attention to me whether checking my chapel attendance or magnifying every little fault and ordering me to see a psychologist, all spelled out in Chapter 6.

> What if you have a toxic boss who routinely blames you for things that aren't your fault . . . In a workplace setting, such injustice can be particularly perplexing: Not only is your livelihood on the line, but workplace politics and the corporate hierarchy can make it difficult for you to get your case heard.
>
> Beverly West, "Neutralize your Toxic Boss"

6

Surveillance and Psychological Testing

More than Paranoia

They're out to get me! . . . Perhaps the key to separating realistic fear from paranoia is the recognition of whether the environment is truly safe or hostile; sometimes this is not initially evident to the clinician . . . [as] when discovering that [an individual] who was thought to be paranoid was indeed being stalked.

James Wilcox

I was in my seminary office getting ready to pack up for the day when a student knocked. I knew him well. He was a good student, one who had taken a few of my courses and we had talked on a number of occasions. I welcomed him in and asked him to sit down. He looked troubled and said that he needed to tell me something. Hesitating a moment, he began disclosing how he'd just had a "very weird" experience. He had been asked to come to Neal's office and was immediately asked about the class he was taking from me and about comments I had made. The student insisted that he had never said anything improper. Neal interrogated him. Still nothing. Neal pressed him further, assuring him, "you will be protected." The student left, having said nothing Neal could add to his case against me. "You will be protected." That was scary for the student and for me.

The student had transferred into the seminary from outside the Christian Reformed Church. He had to chart out some course equivalents and make up some course work that hadn't been credited from the other school. But he was on track to graduate. Now this. He would have been protected if he had been able to come up with some dirt on me. But he hadn't done so. There was developing an atmosphere of fear at the seminary. If you went along with everything the new three-man administration wanted, you were good to go. If not, you might very well pay for it. In this case, however, the student was able to graduate.

Chapel Attendance and Faculty Meetings

As accusations against me piled up, I would learn that the administrators had been filing a list of my faults on such things as my chapel attendance. Who knew that they were keeping a record of the lone female faculty member? I was also cited for leaving Synod early though I had duly asked and received permission for such. But the chapel attendance may have been one of the silliest.

When we think of surveillance, our minds naturally go to hi-tech monitors. I doubt that hi-tech tracking was utilized in this case. In fact, I assume it was old fashioned wandering eyes. Regular attendance was not a requirement for teaching, and several of my colleagues had far more spotty attendance than I did. So why did they pick on me? Had I been steeling paper clips from the copy room, I could have understood the monitoring, but chapel attendance? Yet there it was among other accusations in a summary of my *deficiencies*. But they also nailed me when I actually did attend chapel. One of my colleagues was speaking on a phrase in the Apostles Creed: Jesus descended into hell. Near the end, he remarked that as Jesus was about to ascend into heaven, "he locked the door and threw away the key." I did a double-take thinking that's more like universalism than standard Reformed theology.

Returning to my office, there was a cluster of colleagues complimenting him on his good sermon. As I turned in front of them to enter my office door, I said, "So Jesus locked the door to hell and threw away the key. Sounds like universalism." Before I could get to the next sentence, they howled with laughter. Only a couple of them heard me say without pause, "I wonder what would have happened if I had said that." I opened the door and went in. My colleagues had heard him deliver that line, but none of them noticed or cared because he was obviously very orthodox. So, my comment was funny to them—not to me.

But how could this spark of laughter possibly relate to surveillance? Here is the kicker. At the moment of the burst of laughter, Henry's wife (employed at the seminary) was walking by. I noticed her smiling. She couldn't have known the context, but she heard the laughter. Well, wouldn't you know some weeks later when I wrote again to Henry how difficult it was for me to be sidelined at the seminary, he had a ready response. He wrote back that he had heard how I was laughing and having great fun with my colleagues in the hall outside my office door. So even pillow talk was part of their surveillance.

Was I paranoid, or was I really being watched? In Chapter 2, I cited evaluation comments from #17: "I often find Ruth to be excessively conformist to the predominant faculty ethos, especially when that ethos is negative." I believed that I was being watched when faculty voted. Otherwise, why would #17 know I was being excessively conformist? I would sometimes slide a note to a colleague next to me: "Ask for a ballot vote." Most of the time he didn't, so I would abstain if I suspected my vote would be registered as part of "that ethos" viewed as "negative"—that is, opposed to an administrator's proposal.

A "Threat to Sue Calvin Theological Seminary"

Surveillance documents just kept coming. In one instance I received a memo purportedly written by the facilities director. He was a friend and we often kidded each other about life at the seminary. But tensions were high in 2003 (not entirely because of me) and staff in particular were nervous about their jobs. In this case I had talked with him about a dangerous icy patch near the seminary entry. Three weeks later, I received a memo about my reporting of this problem.

The memo was odd in every respect. My friend's signature was on the bottom, but it wasn't written by him. Across the top in large bold print was written "Memorandum." Who does that? It was formal, with the usual To, From, and Date, sent to Henry (with full name and position), and the so-called writer using his own full name and position as well. The subject line read: "Advise you of threat to sue Calvin Theological Seminary by Ruth Tucker." In the three short paragraphs there are words and phrases my friend never would have used: "subsequent to discussion," "alleviate the disparity," "effecting a permanent solution."

One quote stood out amid the formal tone. "She [that's me] proceeded to say, 'I am going to sue your ass.'" I was obviously kidding. He had apparently mentioned that to another person who told Henry. I showed him the paper and asked if he would read it. He said he didn't even know the meaning of some of the words. He said he didn't remember signing it, but it was his signature. Why, he wondered, would I tell him I was going to sue the school if I hadn't even fallen on the ice? Good question. Henry should have thought of that before insisting he sign the *Memorandum*—or was it a blank page?

I never doubted for a moment that Henry, Neal and Duane were lurking around every corner for *evidence* against me—this Memorandum being one of the documents that they would later submit to the *ad hoc* committee and to the outside independent mediators to prove how unscrupulous I was. Why they couldn't come up with better stuff, I will never know. I truly did have real *deficiencies*.

A "Cat-Fight" in the Student Lounge

Less than a year after the outlandish Memorandum, the facilities director, at my request, sent me an email describing a situation that occurred in the student lounge when no one was around. It related to Henry's "staff member A" and me. "You both appeared angry," he wrote, and the reason he remembered the incident was because he heard her from across the room raising her voice in anger. She and I had been friends. I had learned that she had been talking with Henry. I was very upset when I encountered her and demanded to know what she was telling him. Thus, raising her voice and saying, "I don't want to talk about it." At most this would have been what my colleagues might have described in sexist language, a "cat-fight." Men, of course, argue and raise their voices about important issues. Women have *cat-fights*.

Henry got wind of our encounter and submitted a false *write-up* to the executive board and the faculty status committee (FSC) with no opportunity for me to respond. Had they believed his version, the FSC might have thought I had wrestled her down and beat her head against the floor. That is why I had called upon the facilities director to give his assessment of the situation—a *document* I never used since I had no opportunity to respond to Henry's write-up.

"Staff member A", however, would later contact me about her own awful experience of being *let go* in Neal's office not long after Henry had interrogated her about me. Though she was highly competent in her position, she was told her firing was due to budget concerns. But she held an important staff position and had documented financial misconduct of which the administrators were aware. She was also told that if she said anything negative about what was going on at the school, she would not receive severance pay. She would later email me about our "incident":

> That day when you came to me so upset and said I went behind your back is still very much real with me. Ruth, we were good friends, and the only thing I said to Henry when asked was Yes, when he asked me if you had talked about your re-appointment. . . . Ruth, I am sorry if you feel that I let you down as a friend, I hope you can believe that.

Although the administrators repeatedly said that they wanted me to come back and be part of the seminary community, I believe they purposely kept me sidelined and separated. I have no doubt that Henry was seeking to get dirt on me from this staff member so that he could embellish even the thinnest piece of information. Equally important, he succeeded again in further separating me from a good friend.

Low-Tech Surveillance and Suicide

The "cat-fight" simply didn't cut it as solid evidence against me, so why not send her in for psychological testing. The justification related to a Calvin community *joke*. To relate the convolutedness of the matter would require a chapter in itself, so I tell the tale in abbreviated but even more "scandalous" terms *So, the entire school community is attending a gala where a Rorschach-like symbol is displayed on a large screen. When the crowd moves to the food tables, faculty, staff, students, board members are kidding about seeing a naked lady in the Rorschach.*

The next day jokes continued at faculty lunch time, and, in fact, Henry's quip got the biggest laugh. I had nothing to contribute. As it turned out, the intention of the Rorschach was to symbolize Jesus on the cross. I am certain that none of those who joked or laughed were mocking "our crucified Lord," though Neal would accuse them of doing so, and would make a major case out of it.

More than a year later, the junior colleague in my department had come to my office with a matter related to my situation. I began venting about my frustration with colleagues for not calling for a review of my case. I fumed that I'd come to my wits end, and I picked up on the *joke* of the *naked lady*, saying something like: *I'm so frustrated I feel like running through the halls naked and then throwing myself off the bell tower. Maybe that would get their attention.*

My colleague (whom I hadn't realized at the time had been reporting my *behavior* to administrators) immediately carried my *joke* to Henry. True, I had made an asinine statement, but it was in a private conversation, hardly worthy of being sent along to boards and committees for review. It certainly didn't rank alongside Henry's joke with fifteen faculty sitting around.

Henry, however, would claim this private comment was "what might even be termed gross misconduct." Later, accusing me of having "lapsed into reprehensible conduct and scandalized members of the faculty and staff by it." He also insisted that I would have to see a psychologist because I was suicidal. Now, had I actually followed through and *run through the halls naked*, sure, call it "gross misconduct." But if I followed through by committing suicide, one might think that he would have seen it as tragic rather than scandalous.

Henry had judged my protest against entering the renewal program as "behavior that was clearly inappropriate and that I suspected, at the time, might have been occasioned by a pathological condition or an extreme depression"—behavior that included "sustained soliciting of support from faculty colleagues in a 'battle' against the administration and the Board." It's true that on several occasions I chided colleagues for not supporting a review of my case. But any "pathological" and "sustained soliciting" of them would have been front and center in their second round of evaluations of me. But now matters had gotten serious. My *soliciting* had moved seamlessly to *suicide*.

Psychological Testing

I do not know whether the colleague who reported me or the administrators had ever talked with a suicidal individual (as opposed to a frustrated one). I have. One of my students (an RN in her twenties) whom I knew well, opened up to me about her suicidal thoughts. She had seen therapists and been on and off meds for some years. On one occasion, when we were discussing her terrible battle with depression, I commented on her stellar work in my classes and told her how significant she was in the Calvin community—all true. I asked if there were problems at the seminary related to her depression. No, not at all. She said she simply could not control her awful depression; the meds turned her into a "zombie." *All I long for is peace, and the only way I'll find it is by ending this black depression—by ending my life. You can't know how much I want it all to end.*

She and I met occasionally until she would leave the school a year or so later. I certainly was no more equipped to deal with her situation than were a succession of counselors. In the years since, I have learned of many tragic instances of suicide. I have listened to weeping parents of a very bright young doctor whose black depression, he felt, left him no other choice. In another case, the parents of a brilliant Calvin University senior, top of his class. As I embraced his mother and wept, neither of us had any words.

Had any of the administrators actually believed my flippant comment pointed to my suicide, they might have asked me. Ordering me to see a psychologist was not for my wellbeing. It was one more effort to collect information they could use against me.

My being suicidal was reported to the psychologist as were my other deficits and deficiencies. I was nervous. I had already made a solid case for my teaching capabilities and my relationship with colleagues. Statistics bore me out. I knew I wasn't suicidal, but I had never before been put to the test of sanity. Before I went to the first talk session, a friend commented that she doubted I would be able to pass the tests. Every Calvin student who is ordered to go for testing, she said, ends up at minimum having to go to group therapy. I was doomed.

Our first three 2-hour meetings were talk sessions. In her follow-up letter she summarized our discussions and stated that "it is my clinical judgment that in reality she is neither depressed nor suicidal. Even in the darkest times of her life, Ruth has not seriously considered taking her own life." Three weeks after our talk sessions, I returned to take the Millon Clinical Multiaxial Inventory III. The psychologist stated that "this instrument picked up no significant depression or pathology." She began her summary of the results by stating: "Ruth is a sociable and gregarious woman who presents in a positive manner." She continued with three more descriptive paragraphs, none of which were negative, and she repeated again that "Ruth is neither depressed nor suicidal."

I was elated. I was not a mental case—even after all the school had put me through. The psychologist understood issues related to an all-male workplace: sex discrimination, menopause, hot-flashes and crying. I was incredibly relieved that I was cleared. Neal would have to eat crow. Not quite. He wrote back essentially saying that now I had no excuse for my misconduct. Had the administrators actually thought I was suicidal, one might think that their first response to the report would be one of relief that I was no danger to myself.

Some eight months later in 2004, Neal wrote me a formal letter laying out the conditions of my reappointment that was rubber-stamped by the seminary board. Due to my repeated challenges, my initial one-year terminal appointment was now being augmented with a two-year terminal appointment, that being "at-will employment . . . as a non-tenured faculty member." Only, however, if I met certain—almost-laughable—conditions. The low-tech surveillance yield would serve as a backdrop, including a condition that related to my alleged threatened suicide: "That Prof Tucker not again alarm or threaten to scandalize the seminary community with misbehavior."

Sexism and Charges of Mental Instability

I doubt the administrators had even realized their order for me to get psychological testing was a time-worn sexist power-play. Had it occurred to them, however, it hardly would have made a difference. But if you can prove her *crazy*, it's easier to fire her.

In the midst of her effort to obtain justice from the Australian university where she taught, Professor Judith Bessant tells how she had walked out of the Federal Court to a nearby hospital for a consultation with a surgeon. She had been feeling ill for some months, a condition "doctors put down to a psychological response to workplace stress." She was told to go for counselling and was prescribed meds. More fodder for her university administrators. However, after consulting with the surgeon, she would learn that they had found a "very large," 4 ½ kilo tumor. She would need surgery the next day. After a five-day hospitalization, she was told that it was malignant. She was a mother with young children. She would learn later that it was actually benign. If a man had been ill like she was, would he have been told to take meds and see a counsellor?

Years ago, I began having unbearable headaches. Meds did nothing and I had a six-month old baby to care for. I went to three different doctors, all of whom said essentially the same things: holiday stress. I told them I had no holiday stress; we hardly celebrated the holidays. The throbbing headaches would eventually subside. More than a year later I was telling an acquaintance about my suffering. He told how he had experienced the same thing. He went to his doctor and was asked about his job and hobbies. Turs out he had been painting with clear lacquer in a confined space. That was it, I exclaimed. I was making crafts, brushing lacquer in a small workroom. His doctor was able to remedy the agony. My doctors put me off with what they perceived as a female psychological *disorder*. Whether medical or academic doctors, Judith and I were targets. And employment surveillance would follow us everywhere we went.

Phil Lestmann and the Crooks Running Bryan College

Because of their majority status, sex discrimination is rarely an obstacle for men. But when they are perceived to step out of line for other reasons, they also encounter serious surveillance and harassment in the workplace as Phil Lestmann discovered at Bryan College. In her book, *Evolving in Monkey Town*, Rachel Held Evans offers insights on the school and the town that became famous in 1925 for the Scopes trial.

> What was happening at Bryan College was happening in evangelical schools and churches across the country during the apologetics movement of the 1970's, '80's, and '90's. [It was] born of the necessity to more effectively engage modernism and avoid embarrassments like the Scopes trial.

While seeking to distance itself from its anti-intellectual past, the apologetics movement held tightly to a literal reading of an inerrant Bible. With authoritarian school administrators, the movement often took a toxic turn. When a new administration commandeered the college, it released a revised set of beliefs that all faculty were required to sign. Included were tight restrictions on interpreting the creation account, provoking an uproar that began in 2014. Three years later Marvin Olasky in World Magazine would label it a "Civil war."

The most recent casualty of this war had been Phil, a math professor, department chair with thirty-eight years of teaching under his belt. Hardly someone to intimidate with a smear campaign. It was 10 a.m., July 19, 2017. He had been called to the office of Kevin Clauson, academic vice president. Also present was the vice president of finance. Phil was shown an email and asked if he had written it. Yes. Forget about his nearly four decades of stellar teaching. He was fired. The sentence in question was: "We need everyone to know about the crooks running Bryan." Why didn't I think of that line? I actually said things worse than that, but low-tech surveillance somehow failed to catch it.

Bryan administrators had broken all the rules. Indeed, according to the school's charter, no one, not even the new president and his henchmen, could mess with its statement of faith. Why then would they change it? Was it done in order to rid itself of certain faculty members? Surveillance had opened the door, and firings followed. This was nothing short of administrative mobbing. I will have more to say on "the crooks running Bryan" in Chapter 8.

As for me, I'm convinced that the surveillance and psychological testing had only one purpose—to find evidence to prove that I was shamefully deficient. Shame was the thread that ran through the entire three and a half years that followed the fateful night with Henry. *Does anyone have to know?* More and more, however, I was determined that *yes, people have to know.* But even as I *solicited* my colleagues, thinking they would support me in opening the evidence, they would turn against me. As the next chapter indicates my colleagues engaged in academic mobbing--mobbing incited by an administrative smear campaign.

> A smear campaign, also referred to as a smear tactic or simply a smear, is an effort to damage or call into question someone's reputation, by propounding negative propaganda. . . . A smear campaign is an intentional, premeditated effort to undermine an individual's or group's reputation, credibility, and character.
>
> Wikipedia

7

Academic Mobbing

Colleagues Joining the Posse

Academic mobbing usually begins with an actual but often minor offense that is exaggerated into character assassination.

Jake New

I had not encountered mobbing from colleagues until the administration moved the goalposts and accused me of *ungodliness*, using a variety of terms for it. The rumors and innuendo quickly spread to the faculty. When my one-year terminal appointment had begun to run out, I was permitted to reapply. Many colleagues now believed I deserved my punishment. If Neal had suggested I was guilty of a *very bad* and *confidential* sin, it must be true, they reasoned. Because of surveillance and false accusations, I was sidelined, no longer going to the faculty room for lunch. Henry had urged me to return and warn colleagues not to go "over-the-line."

I had gotten good evaluations the previous year, though discredited by Henry's dishonest summary. But this time around Henry decided to assault me even before he wrote his summary. I was shocked that he would stoop so low. On January 7, 2004, I received a memo from him, written "To Whom it May Concern." "Re: Evaluations of Ruth A. Tucker," addressed to "Colleagues," containing one sentence: "Attached are the faculty colleagues' evaluations of Ruth Tucker with names, signatures, and

71

clear identification removed." It was an outrage, and no one even bothered to care.

The administrators knew exactly what they were doing. It was unlawful, but they knew they could get away with it. I could have gone to court but they had deep pockets. What they did was a clear violation of employment law. "Employee files, which include sensitive employee information, must be kept confidential by HR. Among confidential types of information are 'Assessments or reports.'" They were exhibit A of academic mobbing. Where was that claim to *confidentiality?* I had asked that *all* documents be opened, not just ones condemning me.

Second Round of Faculty Evaluations

Most of my colleagues cited confusion about my being given a terminal appointment and removed from tenure track. For example, one wrote: "she has understandably withdrawn and/or avoids conversations with her colleagues which might be misinterpreted." Another comment: "The faculty was asked to place a tremendous amount of trust in the administration with regards to the events surrounding Ruth. This trust has been given but the result was a disconnecting on Ruth's side from the faculty." Still another: "But if you, Henry, and Neal both agree that there are real problems, I trust your judgment. Still, the whole chain of events is rather amazing to me."

Henry's summary quoted them—that I had been "curt and aloof," that I do not "meet the requirements regarding 'sound judgement,' being 'well-balanced,' and 'excelling in the basic Christian virtues of honesty and humility.'" He had not numbered the evaluations, as he had previously, but I assumed #17 enjoyed crafting his. My colleagues knew that I wanted the evidence opened up. They could have come together *en masse.* But I was an outsider, not a Dutch member of the CRC. And I was a woman. They failed me with "I trust you guys." Worse than that, without knowing the term, they took part in that alarming sport of *academic mobbing.* Why? It's time-consuming and stressful to challenge administrators, and there are prized perks available in academia to keep scholars satisfied.

Cover-Up of Unwanted Sexual Advances

Not only had Henry sought out students he claimed maligned me, but he also sought a retired colleague. Identified by Henry as "faculty member

B," he said that I had been very angry with him—a fair accusation. He had often come to my office uninvited. On one occasion I asked him if he had heard anything about my situation. He said the only one he had talked with about me was Mel (who had berated me in my *renewal program*). I asked what Mel had said. He gave a vague response and insisted that they had talked about me on only one leg of the Iowa bike race. Really. Only one day-long leg. I was very upset that this so-called mentor would be talking about my situation.

Henry, in his review to the executive board, would write that he had apologized to B for my bad behavior. I emailed Henry, requesting a meeting to hear my response to his review. Neal was also present. Not wanting to face them alone, I asked my division chair to be there as well. Included in my lengthy response (January 27, 2004) was this paragraph:

> B came to my office as he often has. . . . I have been uncomfortable with the way he has physically expressed himself, but not wanting to hurt his feelings, I've never directly confronted him. . . . But even after my treating him as badly as he describes, he came over to give me a prolonged hug before he left. I pushed my chair back as far as it would go, and tried to hold him at bay by high-fiving him, but he grabbed my hand as I did so, and then reached down and put his other arm around me and held me. He has made me very uncomfortable on many occasions—one in particular when he pinned me against a door as I was trying to leave, and with his arms around me he told me he loved me and he kissed me while I was pulling away from him. I do not now have—nor have I ever had—romantic feelings toward him

Neal was furious. He didn't believe me. Henry asked me why I had not immediately reported his behavior—if what I was saying were actually true. I responded that I never felt myself to be in actual danger and that I had wrongly assumed that if I were very unpleasant, he would leave me alone. I actually did feel sorry for him, knowing he was lonely and depressed. Since Henry had raised the issue of B in his overview to the executive board, I wanted to respond to this and other issues he had raised. My division chair agreed with me. But a few hours after that meeting, Henry sent me a threatening email: "if you appeal, you will harm yourself and your cause. We will inform the Executive of this opinion . . . prior to the Executive deciding whether or not to receive your presentation." I read the writing on the wall, and backed down.

Both Neal and Henry had questioned the truthfulness of my charge against faculty member B. So also would members of the faculty status committee, one suggesting I had made it up to counter B's charge against me. It is true that I would not have reported B had Henry not raised the issue, but why should that invalidate my claim? Moreover, I do not believe that B went to Henry to report my *bad behavior.* Henry was on another fishing expedition and had a nice perk to offer. Retired B wanted Henry to again assign him to teach his favorite church history course.

Faculty Status Committee

The faculty status committee (FSC) would also receive a copy of Henry's review to the executive board. This committee did not appear out of thin air. In fact, it might have been named for me since it was because of my situation that the committee was formed. I would later write extensive notes on this aspect of my long ordeal.

Faculty meetings were scheduled on the last Friday of the month, always ending with a time of sharing and prayer. One after another clockwise around the U-shaped setting, some colleagues spoke while others passed as I typically did. In the March meeting, less than three months after I had been terminated, one of my colleagues spoke up for me, referencing the accusation of ungodliness against me, a charge already widely rumored among the faculty. He strongly supported me against the administration's false accusations.

Then all but one of my tenured colleagues made statements in my behalf. Some of their comments were shockingly strong—from ones I would have least expected. Henry was absent from this memorable meeting. But when Duane's turn arrived at the head table he said he was astonished that this confidential matter of my ungodliness had been raised and divulged to the entire faculty. He kept repeating himself, holding the floor. Barely had he come to a pause when I jumped in saying I wanted these accusations divulged—that they were not confidential.

I would later learn that both Neal and Duane joined my colleagues for beers after that faculty meeting, something they had not previously done. They apparently didn't want my colleagues to hatch a take-over in their absence. I was told that some "very strong statements were made on my behalf at that time." In an email to a colleague at another school I wrote: "I had thought that things had improved for me since last Friday when all but one of the tenured faculty spoke strongly for me in the faculty meeting, but they've used that against me and are now saying that it's my fault that the morale is so awful among the faculty."

Before that faculty meeting had ended, a colleague suggested that there should be a faculty committee set up to deal with this matter. This was the origin of the faculty status committee composed of three male colleagues. Neal would attend the meetings (as was his privilege for all committees). Indeed, from behind the scenes the three administrators were in control, feeding the FSC with rumors and false statements. I was not interviewed by the committee, nor was I permitted to respond in any way to the false charges. Indeed, the FSC became an academic-mobbing tool of the administration. The three colleagues might have refused to sit on such a committee, but they did not.

Benefits and Perks of Mobbing

There was a window of time after that faculty meeting when my tenured colleagues could have come together and demanded that my case be opened up—forcing the administrators to show their cards. They did not, and instead would join in the mobbing, if not actively, certainly by their silence.

In addition to the FSC, another tool used by the administrators was benefits—buying off colleagues. The perks in academia are endless, from extended sabbaticals and funds for projects to premature promotions and tenure. Most of these happened behind the scenes with notices buried in board meeting notes as though they were routine. I am not suggesting here that there was an obvious *quid pro quo*, but the exchange was understood. One of my colleagues whom I had not known well had surprised me with his strong support during that faculty meeting. I summed up his comments that afternoon: "He said he was shocked to hear the news—that he had very serious questions about a process that could do such a thing to a colleague and he said that he wished something could be done to restore his confidence in the process."

Two months later at the faculty meeting, he lauded Neal for his decision to stay at the seminary instead of accepting the presidency of Princeton Theological Seminary (PTS). Neal thanked him, and nothing more was said. I did a double take. I had worked closely on an editorial board with a PTS professor who served on that school's presidential search committee. I asked him about Neal—Cornelius Plantinga, Jr. He had never heard of him, commenting that there were hundreds of names that had been nominated for the position. The only names he paid any attention to were those who had responded with a vita and a list of references. Neal was not one of them.

It reminded me of years earlier when I had been nominated by who knows to be provost of Wheaton College. I learned of it only when I received a large embossed envelop and letter of congratulations, requesting that I apply for the position. I didn't, but I did save the letter just in case I ever wanted to shamelessly impress someone. I would later learn that my colleague who had congratulated Neal had gotten a nice extension of his sabbatical. With no mention of that, I informed him that Neal had not turned down the PTS presidency. He shrugged and said he had apparently misunderstood. That's believable, but Neal failed to clarify it at that faculty meeting. It would have been the honest thing to do.

The most blatant buy-off of a colleague, however was announced by Duane during a faculty meeting. It was so weird it might have been funny: the promise of a named professorial chair to a non-tenured colleague, hired after I was, who had barely begun his doctoral work. It was a direct slam aimed at me. Had there been funds for a named chair in my department, and had I not been terminated, I would have been the obvious recipient. It was a farce, and everyone in the room surely knew it. Duane's words left us all mute. As it turned out, the idea went nowhere. It may have temporarily boosted the ego of my colleague who had provided "dirt" on me. He was expendable, however. Soon after I left, I would learn that he had *resigned—to go in a different direction.*

Signing off on "Ungodly" Behavior

Fast forward to a session in October of 2005 while Neal and I were being interrogated by outside independent mediators. In a surprise move, Neal would brandish a new "very important" document. I was startled because he seemed to be acting as though this piece of paper was a slam-dunk, proof of his innocence. Addressed: "To Whom It Concern," it was worded as though written by four of my colleagues, stating that Neal "gathered us to ask one question": "When the four of us met with him in January of 2003 to inquire into the status of our colleague Ruth Tucker, had Neal in any way described Ruth, or Ruth's behavior, as 'ungodly'? Had that word, or its cognates been used at all?" Their answer was "To the best of our recollection . . . No." Then on four blank lines, with their full names and titles below were their signatures.

Until Neal pulled this one-page paper with seven lines of text out of his magician's hat, I had not even known my four colleagues had marched in formation to see him. At least they had cared enough about me to do that. Furthermore, I had never claimed he had told them in person that I was ungodly. I might have dismissed the document out-of-hand because it wasn't properly notarized, but I didn't.

What I found curious, however, were the lines that followed their *No*. They reported that "Neal would not reveal anything about the reasons for Ruth's changed faculty status [terminal appointment, removal from tenure track]. He said only that there were reasons and that they were good ones."

What if, at this point, barely two weeks after I had been fired, Neal had chosen to *save face*. When my colleagues marched in to consult with him, he could have stopped everything in its tracks. He could have shifted the blame, telling them that his fellow-administrator Duane had submitted a disparaging *faculty* evaluation of me and that Henry used his negative statements to justify my termination. Neal might have asked them how they felt about that and let them help him decide what to do with this lone woman among them. I am certain of the outcome. The whole pitiful scenario could have ended then and there. Neal could have put his foot on the brake. He didn't. With eyes wide open he continued his assault full throttle down the road of mendacity.

When Neal showed this signed paper to the mediators, I assumed he was seeking to intimidate me and impress the mediators. He did succeed with me, but I well recall how both mediators glanced through the seven lines and set it aside, as though it didn't amount to a hill of beans. They had already seen documents written by him accusing me of "ungodly conduct." Why would this statement make a difference? And did my colleagues sign under duress? It almost appeared that way, though they were all tenured and they certainly could have manned-up and said that they wanted no part in his charade. They didn't. Once again, the term is academic mobbing. Guilty as charged.

My four colleagues had signed on the dotted line that to the best of their recollection they had not specifically heard Neal use any form of the word ungodly when they met with him in January of 2003. They did concede, however, that he said there were reasons "and they were good ones." They also knew that rumors of my ungodliness were flying around at the time they spoke with him and they knew I wanted all documents opened up. If they had not set out on this path of "academic mobbing," as they actually did, thousands of hours needlessly expended could have been avoided—thousands of hours wasted by colleagues, administrators, board members, *ad hoc* committee, independent outside mediators, eventually students—and by me.

Academic mobbing is nothing like a street mob of hoodlums that might attack a police car, as Anson Shupe, has pointed out: A workplace mob often involves only a small group, rarely more than a dozen. It is "usually bloodless and polite." These "mobs often act slowly, over months or years" and it "brims with pretense, subterfuge, and sophistry." The title for Shupe's work is, "When the Bastards Grind you Under."

Calvin Seminary Board Mobbing

I believe that the gross dereliction of duty on the part of the seminary board ranks as academic mobbing—even though, as I recall, there was only one academic on the board. That individual was Jack who led the mobbing. The board's dereliction of duty was made plain to me when a friend compared my situation to a similar situation at the CRC affiliated Trinity Christian College in Palos Heights, Illinois (not to be confused with Trinity Evangelical Divinity School). My friend, with an earned doctorate, was on the board when a faculty member appealed an administrative decision to terminate him. Instead of rubber-stamping that decision, the board agreed to hear him out. My friend was chair of a committee that spent long hours reviewing the case from both sides. In the end the professor received a regular appointment with some stipulations.

In my case, the administrators demanded the situation remain "confidential" because they did not want the documents to see the light of day. I was mobbed not only by the administrators and faculty, but also by the seminary board—by their refusal to review my case when I pleaded with them to do so less than two weeks after I had been terminated. And I would be mobbed by the executive committee of the board throughout my long fight for justice.

The Herbert Richardson Case

I first learned about Herbert Richardson in 2003 when a colleague gave me a copy of a volume by Kenneth Westhues. A Canadian scholar, Westhues is recognized for his writings on academic mobbing, the Richardson case the most often cited. My situation was very different from his, but his case sheds light on the topic. With a PhD from Harvard Divinity School and an academic track record, he joined the faculty of St. Michael's College at the University of Toronto. Though a Presbyterian, the Catholic faculty welcomed him on board. Later, however, as the school was shoring up its fidelity to the Church, he was told he must "sign a document pledging a strict adherence to Roman Catholic teachings." The same was required of other professors, but he refused: "You know, this is a little bit silly [as] a Presbyterian minister," he would retort. "You can't put me under the authority of the Catholic bishop."

He maintained that this was the reason for his firing, but there would be other reasons as well. Students reported an angry outburst in class when he "yelled" at his student assistant. Soon after in 1991, his department chair wrote to the dean: "Richardson's behavior was a time bomb waiting to explode." The following year, a vice president told him to "take early retirement—in three weeks." He managed to stay, however, and was given an extended health-related leave.

The charges against him were not cut and dried. He had indeed started his own business, the Edwin Mellen Press, housed in his basement initially publishing PhD dissertations. As that business grew, colleagues and administrators accused him of using sick leave for publishing purposes. He was ordered to resign or face a public tribunal. He chose the latter which began in 1994. More than a dozen charges were leveled against him, including his failure to close a window after class on a cold night and to erase the blackboard. Colleagues had also discredited his *business* as a vanity press. (I beg to differ. Some of the most valuable volumes in my library were published by Edwin Mellen.)

In the end the tribunal found him guilty on two counts: "abusing his medical leave and not 'fully' disclosing the amount of time he was spending on Edwin Mellen business." He lost his case and was fired. "As I look at the cast of characters who jointly accomplished [his] elimination," writes Westhues, "not one could accurately be described as a bully. In personal manners, they come across . . . as academics equally as civil, polite and well-spoken as Richardson himself. They are without a doubt as normal as any of the rest of us." But they judged him guilty and wanted him out—a case perhaps, as Westhues has suggested, of academic envy.

Mobbing? Are You Kidding?

Although I never accused colleagues of "mobbing," if I had they would have found the allegation ludicrous. They were largely silent, and whenever they did speak, it was "bloodless and polite," with few exceptions. But the mobbing did "brim with pretense, subterfuge, and sophistry." Not all the attributes in my case, however, fit Anson Shupe's framework cited above. Most importantly the administrators had no well-planned "step-by-step" scheme. In fact, it was very clumsily executed from day one. It's hard to picture them huddling in a smoked-filled room planning my firing out ahead of time. (Actually, only one of them smoked.) Henry, I am certain, would not have fired me without having been told to do so. And my colleagues were not mobbing to get rid of me—rather to get me to comply and remain on the faculty.

Indeed, colleagues had no plan at all to rid themselves of me. As to the administrators, their plan was bungled from the beginning. Did one of them ask: *Can we really get away with this? What if she doesn't go quietly? She's a writer, you know. What if she files a law suit? What if the faculty demands answers? What if this drags on for months—or years?*

Did they ever consider the downside of handing me hundreds of documents? Indeed, if they had only interacted with me verbally, they would have avoided my document defense. And, since they started my firing process with no regard for protocol, why did Henry cave in when I asked to see actual faculty evaluations? That set them up for the "smoking gun"—the obvious charge of flagrant dishonesty? Once the process had begun, did they try to coordinate their falsehoods? There was little evidence of that. In fact, inconsistent fabrications were evident in one document after another. It's possible that one very clever individual might have quickly succeeded in ridding the school of me. But inconsistent falsehoods multiplied by three only muddied their claims—their plot to fire me proving utterly inept.

Not that my response was *ept*. When I look back now, more than a dozen years later I think of many things I should have done differently. And I wonder why I would have asked that pitiful question of Henry: *Does anyone have to know?* Why wouldn't I have stood up defiantly and said, *you'll hear from my lawyer.* It's true that, before having seen the numbered faculty evaluations, I had somehow assumed Henry was being truthful. But that's not a good excuse. I should have kept a clear mind instead of falling apart. I fault my colleagues, however, more than myself. Had they demanded a review, the board could have engaged outside independent mediators right away instead of waiting nearly three years. As it was, I would seek outside consultation, with no support from them. That action would set off a firestorm and trigger retaliatory harassment as the next chapter shows.

Retaliation is any adverse employment action an employer takes against the complaining employee because of the fact that he or she complained. The U.S. Supreme Court has declared that any negative act towards the complaining employee can constitute retaliation.

Alyson Brown, "Revenge Isn't Always Sweet"

8

A Mothers' Day Letter

Unbridled Anger Leading to Mediation

It is against the law to punish someone for complaining about discrimination or harassment. The most obvious forms of retaliation are termination, discipline, demotion, pay cuts, or threats to do any of these things.

"How to Handle Discrimination
and Harassment Complaints"

In January of 2004, one year after the seminary board had rubber-stamped Neal's decision to remove me from tenure track and give me a terminal appointment, the board was meeting again for another rubber-stamping ceremony. Most of my colleagues had been taking part in mobbing primarily by their silence, refusing to even listen to my plea for the evidence be opened up. By this time students were finding out. One older student showed me seminary board minutes that reported four of my colleagues were being promoted. For me: "attorney-approved expectations and requirements for continuing employment." My student said he wanted me to know that many other students had seen it, copied it and were talking about it. I believe the administrators wanted to spread the word that the board and lawyers had supported them in crushing me.

Despite the rumors flying through the student body, I carried on in my classes and tried to be as engaging and fun-loving as I had been before that fateful night. Indeed, my student evaluations clearly improved. If a professor is not already engaging, it's difficult to suddenly become so. From that standpoint I changed little. But in one respect, I changed a lot. How does a professor improve evaluations? It's obvious. Teach to the evaluations. How else could I have risen to second highest of all those who were evaluated during the term right after I had been terminated? I began studying blank evaluations and began teaching accordingly. Some evaluation questions seemed odd to me. But I did what I had to do.

Blissful Spring Days of 2004

As the bitter winter rolled into a Michigan spring, the terrible loneliness of being sidelined by my colleagues began to ease. Then on a spring day in late April, I opened my church history class by saying I had a little announcement to make. I told students I was engaged to be married. It was a fun class and the students, as usual, were very personal and interactive. They cheered and asked questions. One student asked if I would show my engagement ring. I said that my fiancé (John Worst, Professor emeritus at Calvin College) had not gotten me one—that he'd gotten me real estate instead.

There was a gasp, and I'll never forget that student in the back row. He was a Methodist minister. He shouted out, where is it? I said west of Grand Rapids. He was incredulous (as though he were the set-up straight man). I drive in from the Muskegon twice a week. How far west? I said about ten miles on Highway 45. Where? he asked, without missing a beat. I paused, as though I didn't want to tell. Then I said: Rosedale Cemetery. The class howled with laughter. I explained. John had three plots, two where lie buried his dearly departed wives and one for himself. When he asked me to marry him, he wondered aloud if he could purchase the adjoining plot for me. The students were still snickering. I said, don't laugh; it cost him $640. It is real estate. How many brides-to-be get a gift like that!

Colleagues and administrators would learn only after students spread the news. John and I were married in late August in a small back-yard family ceremony. Only one of my colleagues (with his wife) would be invited to our reception some weeks later, after our honeymoon to Scotland. I had been scheduled to speak there, and it doubled as the perfect time away together.

With my engagement and marriage to John, Neal appeared to have a rather sudden change of attitude toward me. John was a professor at the college across the drive. He was Dutch, born and bred CRC, and highly regarded. Neal had known of him and was no doubt somewhat surprised when he learned. Things could have significantly improved for me at that time had I ignored the previous fifteen months, re-entered the faculty room and pretended nothing had happened. I was almost their equal, now to be married to an insider.

I am not, however, calibrated that way. I had never imagined that marrying a wonderful man would solve my terrible problems at the seminary. In fact, as John read through all my documents and learned on a daily basis how I was being treated, he was outraged. Some days he wanted me to carry on with my fight for justice; other days, he wanted me to resign. But I would *carry on with my fight*, as the administrators had repeatedly accused me of doing. And John supported me every step of the way.

More Students Learn About my Situation

A surprising number of students approached me saying how upset they were about my situation, many of whom were Koreans. I had been to Korea, toured a number of cities and spoke (with a translator), at several conferences. I love kimchi. In fact, students sometimes brought me their own version of that delightful Korean dish, which I tasted first in the kitchen of my Korean sister-in-law. Three of my texts had been translated into Korean, and I was often asked to sign copies. So, when they learned of my terrible situation, word spread quickly with great sadness among the entire community.

One day two young Chinese women came to my office. I invited them in to sit down. No. They wanted to tell me something and began repeatedly saying *so sorry*. They said they hoped that I would keep teaching. They said I was *very good teacher*. I could wish I had an audio recording of their words. It brings tears to my eyes even now recalling those few minutes. They were almost talking over each other with the same words—two young women dear to my heart having difficulty expressing words from their hearts in a second language.

On June 23, 2004, I wrote in my CTS Journal:

I can't get away from my situation here at CTS. Just minutes ago, one of my Indonesian students, stopped in my office to return a book; I asked her to sit down and we chatted about her folks coming this summer, etc. Then she asked if I were leaving the seminary—saying that there had been a rumor among the students that I had problems here and was leaving. My blood pressure rises every time something like this happens—that it's now out among students that there is something deficient about me. She commented that she hoped I didn't leave—that all the students like me so much.

This is not to imply that American and Canadian students didn't come by to express their anger about my situation. But Asians, from my experience, respect authority more than do westerners. For them there was a serious conflict of loyalty—teacher vs administrator. They were students who stood by me with deep sadness, no cynicism.

"We Didn't Handle That Situation Well"

Henry would never have admitted that he didn't handle my situation well. But he could say that about another faculty sacking some years before he became academic dean. I became aware of this situation soon after I joined the faculty. In fact, this man's leaving the school had opened a faculty position for me. He had been up for tenure, but certain professors opposed his theological views. Fast forward to the fall of 2004, a ministry division lunch meeting to interview a candidate for a part-time position. At one point the candidate, aware of my situation, asked about the morale at the seminary. Henry answered in a vague round-about way, saying that my predecessor had left the seminary "under a cloud," adding "We didn't handle that situation well." I apparently looked at him *as though he were from Saturn*, as I wrote in my CTS Journal:

> I looked at him in stunned disbelief, and he said, "why are you looking at me as though I were from Saturn," and I responded, "Well, wasn't [he] given mediation?" Henry responded in the affirmative.

Later that day I inquired of a colleague, again writing in my journal: "He said that [the] CRC Director of Pastor Church Relations met with [my predecessor] and the Theology Division three times." My predecessor was in the ministry division and had openly interpreted ecclesiological issues that several in the theology division found unacceptable. In the end, however, before he accepted a position at another seminary, he was granted tenure despite some faculty disapproval.

I would occasionally see my predecessor at professional meetings. He was pleased with his new situation, and he felt very bad about what I was going through. He was surprised that this faculty-run seminary had so quickly been taken over by a three-man administration.

In Search of Faculty Votes

I made further entries in my "CTS Journal" in late 2004, that points to this turn away from a faculty-run institution:

> [Duane], in the [ministry division] meeting proposed that we send no faculty candidate (replacement for retiring Bob DeVries) to the full faculty so as to leave the door open for gender diversity—that he's always been on record for that, and that if Ruth Tucker is absent from the faculty, we are "all a bunch of white men."

I had not heard my *absence* so brazenly stated as Duane did in front of my colleagues. He apparently wanted to be on record favoring gender equity. He put forth the name of a woman well-known in CRC circles, though unqualified for the open position. His insistence did not fly with the division, and a male professor outside the CRC was voted in by the faculty. At the next full faculty meeting, Duane called for a woman on staff to be promoted to faculty status—again, claiming gender diversity. The faculty voted it down. I wrote in my Journal:

> I am also seeing something else in this that I have known but have not clearly articulated before—that the Administration is doing anything it can to get a majority voting bloc, and [she] is an obvious candidate for this.

Duane would fail in these efforts to appoint "friendly" women who were unqualified for open positions. He had not been subtle about his contempt for "the faculty," colleagues commenting that he liked to say, "the only F-word in my vocabulary is faculty."

Continued Appeals for Mediation

By the end of 2004, things had gotten no better at the seminary. Dear husband John was patient and opened a thousand doors for us to have fun together. But I needed outside help. I made an appointment with Dr. Linda Hertel-Dykstra (the psychologist I was required to see in 2003), informing her that my situation had only gotten worse. She strongly advised mediation.

I emailed Henry telling him that I had visited her some months earlier "and again on the phone last week," and that she strongly recommended mediation "conducted by someone who is familiar with neither side and who has gender sensitivity." He emailed back saying, among other things, "please know that I am not insensitive to what you describe as your pain and anguish. My prayers will be with you today and in the coming days."

How many days and how many administrators does it take to change a light bulb—or, in this case, to write a formal 12-line letter? Indeed, Henry responded to my request for mediation, not once but twice—his second response very different:

> You ask whether I will agree to mediation. There are no recommendations on the table, no decisions to make. The matter of your reappointment is not before us at this time and that will not be until next academic year. Two years ago you wrote, "I will enter a program of renewal in good faith." Therefore mediation is not an option.

He added: "We are there for you, and we wish for you to flourish in our midst." He goes on to say that he does not understand why I would "speak of punishment of . . . extreme severity."

The administrators surely knew the significance of tenure. In 2007, there was a news story about a college in Grand Rapids that was planning to phase out tenure. In light of this, the Calvin College provost Claudia Beversluis commented: "A tenure track appointment is the most highly sought appointment. . . . People will leave other places if they can get a tenure track appointment. It's longer term job security." My removal from tenure track was *punishment of extreme severity.*

Asking for Assistance from AAUW

By the spring of 2005, I was convinced that I could not find justice within the seminary or the CRC. In the meantime, I had discovered a thin book entitled *Tenure Denied* published by the American Association of University Women (AAUW). As I studied the text, I was hopeful that here I might find assistance. I contacted the local branch leader who invited me to join the organization. After attending several meetings and talking with Melissa, one of the officers, she agreed to submit my written complaint when she attended the State Convention in May.

At about the same time, I met with Peter Borgdorff, Executive Director of the CRC, asking him to help me get mediation by appealing to Sid Jansma, seminary board president. Among the documents I gave Peter was the summary I had sent to Melissa on sex discrimination—a summary that featured specific facts, including a comparison with a colleague. He had been promoted to associate professor, while I had been demoted:

- I have a Ph.D. (1979, Northern Illinois University); he is working towards one.
- I have 2+ decades teaching experience; he came in as a new teacher.
- I have written 17 books (with 15 foreign-language translations), many scholarly articles, and have a publisher-sponsored website; he has no books, a few short church-related writings.
- I am president of my professional association, Association of Professors of Mission (2005); he is not even an active member.
- I serve on the governing board of the American Society of Missiology; he is not active in the organization—though it is directly connected to his field.
- I have served in the local church, denomination, and community (above average, I believe, among colleagues); he has done very well in this area.
- I ranked 2nd highest among faculty on student evaluations; he ranked [status withheld] based on an overview mistakenly attached to my evaluations

If my credentials had been placed alongside his (without name or gender), I have no doubt that an objective review would have ranked me higher. This was a clear case of sex discrimination. After looking over my several pages, Peter asked if he could pass it on to Neal for his response. I told him I had no objection. I had done nothing wrong.

The Grounds-for-Termination Letter

Back in January of 2003, barely two weeks after I had been terminated, I had been advised to write to Sid, board president, asking for the board's grounds for *rubber-stamping* (though I didn't use that term) the administrators' decision. I did that, but I never heard back—no "grounds." The *Mothers' Day* letter of May 2005, however, was filled with "grounds."

Within days after receiving the summary of my situation that I'd sent to Melissa and passed on by Peter, Neal ordered me to come to his office to receive a letter. Not in my mail box. Not from his secretary. In fact, she scheduled the exact time at which I was to arrive. I understood this as harassment. I was nervous. I don't recall any spoken words. I do recall his expression of intense anger. That was late Friday afternoon. John and I were leaving town for a much-needed getaway. I was tempted to set it aside until Sunday night. However, I did not. But I have since referred to that five-page screed as Neal's Mothers' Day Letter.

Here he referenced Melissa's name no less than fifteen times. Of all people, someone I barely knew who had served merely as a messenger. Six times he threatened me in bold print: "This violation is a ground for termination." Most of his rant related to "confidentiality" issues. For example, I had written in my overview that the administration had repeatedly tried to silence me—to "seal the environment." He did not deny that quote. Rather: "But the document in which I used that language was confidential, and your quoting it to Ms. [name withheld] is therefore a violation of Requirement 2 above ['That Prof. Tucker respect and maintain boundaries of confidentiality.'] Again, "This violation is a ground for termination."

He also wrote:

> Melissa [name withheld] must wonder indeed about an institution in which a female faculty member innocently requests reappointment and the administration replies by accusing her of combativeness. [Actually, saying I was "putting on some boxing gloves."] Your suggestion to her that this is what happened is an injurious distortion of the facts, and your accusation of sexism, based upon this distortion, is therefore reckless and a violation of requirement of 3 above. **This violation is a ground for termination.**

Again, he wrote that my summary for Melissa "also distresses me because it is so damaging to the reputations of the [3 named administrators] as well as to the reputation of Calvin Theological Seminary." He accused me of giving Melissa a very one-sided summary because "it doesn't mention provisions by the Administration and Board for personnel to support you, personnel with whom to share confidential information, the lengthy and numerous meetings in which prayers and kindness were extended for and to you." True, I should have told Melissa how they put me in a "renewal program" with Mel and Jack in order to "preserve [my] dignity" and about all the other meetings I was required to attend to deal with my *ungodliness* and all the prayers they had offered up in my behalf.

Neal's letter is an example of what is termed retaliatory harassment: "any adverse employment or educational action taken against a person because of the person's participation in a complaint or investigation of discrimination or harassment of any kind." That standard is now part of the new code: "Calvin Seminary is prepared to take appropriate steps to protect individuals who fear they may be subjected to retaliation." Very interesting.

Emboldened by Peter, I responded to Neal's Mothers' Day Letter in strong terms:

> You seem to argue that material marked "confidential" cannot be disclosed by the recipient. I disagree with that view. In fact, I believe the term "confidential" should not be employed to silence an individual. I have alleged sex discrimination from the very beginning. . . . Utilizing a stamp of CONFIDENTIAL does not protect sex discrimination any more than it would protect sexual harassment or any other kind of abuse.

Even though I sounded courageous, I was nervous as a cat. I had experienced Neal's seething anger on earlier occasions, and I found it very unsettling. I immediately copied Neal's letter for Peter, telling him about my distress and asking if he would intervene. He did, and from that point on things temporarily cooled off. Neal's letter demonstrated how matters can be muddled when three administrators are together mobbing an individual. In my response, I had challenged his charge that I failed to maintain "boundaries of confidentiality," and cited an email (3-22-03):

> Those boundaries, however, do not preclude me from sharing information with individuals about my situation and asking for their advice and help. Henry wrote to me about this in reference to the "renewal" program I was required to enter. "You are, of course, free to confide in anyone you wish, but in the more 'formal' process the advocate should be an 'insider.'"

"CTS and I have grave concerns." This was a phrase Neal used in a formal letter to me some three weeks after he had written the "Mothers' Day" letter. His use of the term "CTS and I" is very telling, as though he spoke for the entire seminary community. So, what did "CTS and I" have grave concerns about? He continued: "what we view as numerous violations by you of the terms the Board set for your continued employment at CTS"—in other words, *my seminary*.

Teaching at Bryan College in "Monkey Town"

There are various ways to railroad professors out of their teaching careers. One is to add new charges and move the goal posts: in my case from student and faculty evaluations to *ungodliness*. Another is to ignore protocol on such matters as warning her of an impending firing and threatening her if she seeks to make a legitimate appeal. Still another way is to tighten up the school's religious beliefs—and for those who refuse to sign on the dotted line, show them the door. That is what professors at Bryan College in Dayton, Tennessee, confronted.

In this case, President Stephen Livesay would survive, despite a no-confidence vote of the faculty of 30-2. Some refused to sign the new *statement of faith* and were forced out, while others, desperately needing to save their jobs, signed. Math professor and department chair Phil Lestmann, as mentioned earlier, sent an email and was caught red-handed after someone ratted on him by revealing the offending sentence: "We need everyone to know about the crooks running Bryan." Without even letting him explain what kind of a gang of crooks they were, two top administrators on that July morning of 2017 ended his nearly four decades at the school.

As was true of Neal's Mothers' Day letter, the grounds for Lestmann's termination were spelled out in no uncertain terms, as Marvin Olasky has written:

> The grounds: "violation of multiple policies including our Community Life Standards and Disparagement Policy," which states, "Public disparagement of the college, its policies, mission, purpose, personnel, and/or doctrine is not acceptable." Bryan's Faculty-Administrative Guide says tenure is no protection against "gross insubordination."

I was guilty of "gross misconduct," he of gross insubordination." Hard to say which is worse, but he was fired on the spot for his. I would be permitted to carry on for more than three years. Had he been willing to leave early, he could have collected a half-year's salary—on the condition that he not speak ill of the college and say that the separation was by mutual agreement. He refused the "hush money" and spread the word about what had happened. Within a week he had gone public with an online petition calling for the ouster of the president and the chair of the board.

Some 1800 signed the petition, a significant number since the school had barely more than a third that many students. Phil is one of my heroes. We each wear the accusations against us—gross insubordination and gross misconduct—as a badge of honor. He was determined to go public and get the word out beyond the halls of Bryan College. My little effort to make an appeal through AAUW would accomplish little except set the stage for an accusation of hysteria—and for mediation—as the next chapter demonstrates.

> As many around the world have now seen or heard, Senator Kamala Harris, Democrat of California, was interrupted for the second time in a week by her male colleagues, and called "hysterical" for behavior that is clearly, undeniably not hysterical but forceful and assertive.
>
> Kathy Caprino, "Gender Bias at Work"

9

Hysterical Woman

35 Minutes of "Incoherent Rage"

Hysteria was declassified as a mental disorder by the American Psychiatric Association in the 1950s, and thankfully there is, at present, no legal defense for locking women in the attic and calling the exorcist. But what has persisted across generations is the desire to shame those who challenge authority as disturbed and diseased.

Alison Espach

What if the accusation of "ungodly" conduct (understood by all concerned to be sexual misconduct) turned out to be a completely bogus smear campaign? What if Neal had not even heard rumors of my being a slut? What if he moved the goal posts and claimed, instead of sexual misconduct, I had said some wicked things to him when I was in a meeting? The damage, however, was done. Once rumors are flying about sexual misconduct, it's impossible to take them back. The meaning of "ungodly conduct" did not require a dictionary. Everyone knew. But in case people were not entirely clear, the CRC had put it in writing:

Examples of related ungodly conduct include, but are not limited to, participation in pornography, engaging in sexual contact in return for payment or any other favor, or voyeuristic behavior, displays of sexually offensive material, suggestive gestures and remarks, and other sexually intimidating behavior.

In the spring of 2005, after the executive director of the CRC had fought hard to obtain mediation for me, an *ad hoc* committee of the seminary board of trustees met to consider my case. I wrote to them that it was critical that the committee obtain in writing exactly what Neal's charge of "ungodly conduct" was. He probably wasn't expecting such a demand, but he had no choice. He had to come up with something.

What does a seminary president do? He had not only accused me in print, but also said things to the seminary board, altogether as many as twenty people in one room. Twenty, though even if sworn to secrecy, tell their wives, and on and on. And, of course, faculty members and students quickly find out. So, what does he do? It would seem to me that if he is going to fabricate "notes," he might come up with a juicy sex scandal. The only problem with that is answering the charge with: *Why didn't you send her packing in a heartbeat*, as the former academic dean claimed the punishment would be. *Why did you fail to specify this sex scandal for more than two years?* So, he fabricated notes detailing my alleged hysteria.

But why didn't the *ad hoc* committee ask: *why did you fail to mention this hysteria for more than two years?* The members didn't ask because it would have been too embarrassing for Neal. They should have seen right through his lame effort to come up with something in writing. They should have recognized immediately that he apparently had no scruples about fabricating an enormous lie. But it was a trustee board committee and they were loyal to him.

He would claim that he had previously mentioned two "incidents," and that I knew exactly what these "incidents' entailed. His raising the matter of such incidents came just weeks after that fateful night when Henry terminated me. I was bewildered. One had no corresponding date to my calendar or saved emails. As it turned out, he was several months off. He would later try to alter the date, though still incorrectly. The other incident had no date at all. When I would eventually see his fabricated notes, I was astounded. Neal and I had enjoyed a good relationship during that time frame. He had sent me a congratulatory note about one of my recent books. And on July 18, 2002, soon after this alleged "incident" of raging at him with expletives, he wrote me a friendly, fun-loving note:

Dear Ruth,
I just came out of a 9:30 meeting to get the message about your birthday treats. Sorry I didn't know and wasn't there! But Happy Birthday. I'd come to

your office and sing the song, but that would be too scary for everybody. So, grace and peace instead.

Yours,

Neal

Fabricated Notes

I cite only the most damning paragraph of his "notes." I had been called to a meeting with him and Duane, as I alluded in Chapter 2. According to Neal's newly divulged "notes," Duane asked me a straightforward question as to whether I knew "anything about that"—referring to things I had allegedly said the day before in the faculty room:

> "What followed, without pause, was a <u>tirade</u>—a stream of accusations (of all the sexist tricks, to haul me in here and take me to the woodshed!"), expostulation, and sheer, incoherent rage. I've never in my ministry of thirty-one years witnessed anything like it. All entreaties with entreaty body language ("Ruth, we're trying for a kinder, gentler, ethos. PLEASE help us!) were met with more venom, some of it vulgar (you know where you can shove that!"), and some of it derisive, and all of it motored by one of the single most explosive, out-of-control losses of Christian self-control that I've ever witnessed.
>
> This went on for thirty-five minutes. . . . "

First of all, what happened to his previous charges of "ungodly conduct"? There is nothing in his "notes" that suggest sexual misconduct on my part—nothing more than womanly hysteria.

But beyond that, the paragraph is false in all respects. I previously cited an email I wrote to Neal the day after this meeting proving that these notes were fabricated. But the paragraph is also absurd and contradictory. Why wouldn't he and Duane get up and leave rather than sit listening to me explode for 35 minutes? It does not ring true, and it makes them both appear decidedly pathetic.

What is the meaning of "incoherent rage"? Screaming strings of monosyllables? Again, it doesn't ring true. And, if it is incoherent, why does he include very specific phrases—ones I've never used. Had I done so, I would have been begging to be fired on the spot.

His notes are incorrectly dated, a fact proven by my email the following day. More significantly, the "notes" did not surface until more than two years after the actual meeting when I insisted that he put his accusation of "ungodly conduct" in writing

It's simply beyond belief that Neal would have sat on such notes for more than two years during which time he was trying to defend his firing of me with far less serious accusation such as irregular chapel attendance, leaving a synod meeting early, and petty quoted statements against me by a staff member (who later denied making them).

During the three years after I was terminated, I disputed that decision with dozens of documents. The administration, of course, had documents of its own. It is most telling, however, that none of these documents referenced an alleged tirade. In a long memo of January 28, 2003, less than ten months after the purported "incident" occurred, Neal noted nine of my "deficits and lapses," making no mention at all of a tirade or even of generalized anger issues.

When I was sent to a psychologist, not one word was mentioned about serious anger issues. Indeed, if the description of this hysteria had occurred, why wouldn't he have ordered me to a psychologist the next day?

In fact, he wrote nothing to me on the day of this alleged "tirade" nor anytime afterward. The first time I learned of it was when I received the fabricated notes from the ad hoc committee.

It was not as though the administrators would have been averse to using strong language for my misbehavior. Instead, however, Neal would send me a cute little note about singing to me.

Following his description of female hysteria, Neal wrote a short paragraph:

> This went on for thirty-five minutes. Duane and I said no more than two or three sentences until midway, when I confronted her. "Ruth, you have just spent fifteen minutes assaulting Duane and me in response to his question— his question, not accusation."

Actually, there was an "accusation." Neal began his "notes" by referencing a cancelled chapel speaker, "a decision [I] criticized." He continued: "According to a report by a trusted senior member of the faculty, she attacked Duane and me in the faculty room calling us 'stupid,' 'hicks,' 'power mad.'" I have little recollection of the faculty room discussion on the day he is referencing. However, I have my own notes of the meeting with Neal and Duane, confirming they did raise the issue of the faculty room discussion (though not accusing me then of using such terms.) After I left that meeting, I saw Henry at the community coffee pot, as I recorded in my notes. I asked him how he would describe yesterday's discussion on the chapel cancellation. He said three words: "the usual grousing." (This was months before Henry fired me on that fateful night—when he was still my friend.)

Faculty room interaction typically ranged from "the usual grousing" and debating fine points of theology to bursts of laughter when someone was telling a funny self-deprecating story. Never once did I hear anyone come close to calling a colleague or administrator "stupid," "hicks," "power mad." It would have been so out of line that the individual would have been collectively called out in a heartbeat. Colleagues would have followed up and come to my office and talked with me personally. And they would not have forgotten it when some months later they were writing evaluations of me. Simply put, it did not happen.

A "<u>question</u>, not accusation," had allegedly sparked my first fifteen minutes of hysteria. The fabricated "incident notes" summarize the following twenty minutes in seventy-one words:

> More Assaults.
>
> At the end I said, I think our question has been answered—at least as to your attitude. We're not getting any further, so let's quit./ Again, I beg you to help us with the kinder, gentler Seminary.
>
> She did not walk out, she stormed out.
>
> Duane and I discussed the incident at length. We were both deeply disturbed by it. I am writing it up for the file.

Outside Independent Mediation

Neither the initial *ad hoc* committee nor the later independent outside mediators were given authority to make decisions, only non-binding recommendations. But this first committee to review my case, even with Jack as chair, concluded that the process of firing me had been flawed and that I should get "redress." That word led to the long struggle to obtain outside independent mediation that the administrators fought every step of the way. Nevertheless, a team of two highly recommended individuals were hired. The eight weeks of mediation was truly an ordeal. It was no secret that Board President Sid Jansma, Jr., a wealthy oil *baron*, was paying the hefty cost. His input was sometimes needed, and on at least three occasions, Neal immediately pulled a phone out of his pocket, speed dialed, and was asking Sid within seconds. I found that intimidating. I didn't own a cell phone, much less one that dialed Sid.

After eight weeks of interrogating the four of us, the mediators were pushed for a quick report that would be ready for an executive board meeting soon to follow. I was not optimistic about the outcome. Three powerful men against a terminated woman and her documents. And it was obvious every step of the way what outcome Sid wanted. The meeting date and place were hastily determined. I was tense when I arrived. Present were two mediators, Neal, Duane, Henry, Board president, Sid, Jack and another executive board members , Peter Borgdorff and myself. We all listened intently. I couldn't believe what I was hearing. The mediators had listened to me and read the documents.

I had already been beaten down so much that I feared it would happen again. But the outside independent mediators saw right through the terrible injustice, and solidly came down on my side. The report was read and later faxed and emailed to all parties. There were a lot of words expended for their pay, but here is how I would later sum it up to my colleagues:

> On October 19, 2005, after eight weeks of mediation, Dr. Brink and Ms. Bennett emailed to all parties their report that contained the following 7 statements that I have numbered as follows: 1—"We reached some conclusions which were similar to points made by the Ad Hoc Committee of Review" [particularly "redress" for me]. 2—"We think that if the seminary goes to court, it will probably lose, in part, because Ruth is well documented." 3—"Much more evidence was needed, as well as documentation of non-compliance . . . before her removal from tenure track." 4—"We recommend that Ruth be appointed full professor." 5—"We also recommend retroactive pay to January 2003." 6—"We support the suggestions made by the Ad Hoc Committee for addressing Observed Deficiencies in the Re-Appointment Procedures." 7—"The allegations of 'ungodly' behavior will be deleted and acknowledged by administration to be inflammatory."

A Final Kick in the Face

Their written assessment, of course, was non-binding. But I was ecstatic. I was not prepared to hear such good news. Duane, however, immediately said that the report was supposed to bring the two sides together—focusing on the future not to the past. Not true. From day one the mediation in every session related to why I had been terminated. And the report *did* speak directly to the future—full professor, retroactive pay and more. Their rejection of it was because it did not come down on their side.

Before I realized what was happening, we were split into two groups to talk about how to get along with each other. The three administrators were with a mediator devising a plan by which I could come back on tenure track. They simply regurgitated their previous schemes requiring me to abide by their specifications. But in this instance I would have to sign a non-disclosure agreement, never speaking of their academic assault on me again. By the next day the mediators' report was deep-sixed because Sid would claim the fax was "smudged" and thus invalid.

I later asked Sid: Had the *assessment come down in favor of the administrators, would that smudge have made it invalid?* He simply snorted as though my question were invalid. Actually, Sid was an affable, down-to-earth guy who in other circumstances I would have found compatible. But his bias barred him from being honest and fair.

A Fifteen-Minute Report to Colleagues

In a follow-up meeting with Sid and two board members, and after much haggling, they agreed to call a special faculty meeting to let me speak to colleagues—for a maximum of fifteen minutes. I was well prepared and articulate as I read my tightly-worded statement aloud. It was a short overview of my ordeal, beginning with Henry on that fateful night nearly three years earlier. I chided my colleagues. They were a "curious bunch" but never curious enough to insist my documents be opened up. I gave an overview of the mediators' report, much like the overview above. I ended by saying:

> If I am accused of being selective, that is true. To sum up in 15 minutes some 3 years of meetings and documents is impossible without being selective. I would like you all to see the documents. As for me, I will leave the seminary. I request that my name be removed from the current evaluation process. I will not teach after my terminal appointment runs out.

I don't recall Henry's response. He seemed a bit shell-shocked. Neal was absent due to a fall. Duane quickly took the floor saying this was probably the best decision for all concerned. As to my colleagues, my perception of their betrayal was palpable. They initially reacted in stunned silence. But as astonished as they appeared to be, they were convinced that I could have saved my job if I had really wanted to. I was required to leave the room while Henry, Duane, Sid and the two other board members remained,

Neal on a speaker phone. I was dismissed with no one there to defend me. Standard treatment.

Martin Scharlemann's Playbook

I could have survived had I taken a page from Professor Martin Scharlemann's playbook. He survived by agreeing to three things: causing "disturbance and confusion" at the seminary; secondly, to withdraw his writings; and finally, "asking the church to forgive him."

The setting for Martin was Concordia Seminary in St. Louis, a denominational school of the Missouri Synod Lutheran Church. The school was in chaos and it would prove to be the biggest seminary scandal of the twentieth century. I was a pastor's wife and doctoral student when the news stories broke—news from major outlets dragging out for more than four years. I was also hearing the lament from Kit, a friend and neighbor, a member of the denomination.

Certain top officials at the seminary and in the denomination had added tight restrictions on the teaching of the Genesis creation account (not unlike Bryan College). In the end, the seminary fell apart. "Never have we had forty-five faculty [out of fifty] stand together on an issue," said professor Ralph Klein. "For the teachers, the issue is one of academic freedom to teach the Bible as they see it within the synodical confessions." With five remaining professors and barely two dozen students the seminary would keep going, supported by a few powerful individuals in the denomination. Martin would become acting president. He kowtowed to the authorities and saved his job, though hardly his integrity.

The professors who were forced to leave formed a new seminary, but the denomination refused to permit its students to be ordained. After struggling for several years, it merged with another Lutheran seminary.

The failure of my colleagues to react even after I had spoken for fifteen minutes harks back to the Concordia Seminary situation. Because that seminary had received accreditation, the American Association of University Professors (AAUP) agreed to review the case. John Tietjen, president of the seminary, when he and forty-five faculty members were forced out, commented on the 1975 AAUW report. His words are mine as indicated by brackets:

> [T]he evidence presented by the committee substantiates the conclusion of the report. It is a mark of the tragedy which has befallen Concordia [Calvin]

Seminary that its present faculty and administration, as well as many in The Lutheran Church-Missouri Synod [CRC], will not be disturbed in the least by the conclusion of the AAUP *ad hoc* committee [outside independent mediators].

I was very disheartened that after clearly enunciating how the outside independent mediators' report had so solidly come down on my side, my colleagues were not troubled enough—even at that late date—to cry foul. Indeed, it was "a mark of tragedy" that they appeared not to "be disturbed in the least by the conclusions." In my situation, of course, it was not a vast majority, rather a minority of one forced to leave. They might have stepped up to the plate. My short time limitation, however, did not allow me to summarize the foul ordeal that finally led to mediation.

A Melodramatic Written Request

My colleagues would never know about the months-long battles I fought to obtain a review of my case. The administrators set up roadblocks every step of the way. After I was finally permitted to have a board committee look at my case, Sid asked me to put in writing what I wanted mediated. I might have asked the committee to make a determination on sex discrimination, but I wanted to make it simple and straightforward.

I responded with two written questions: Was I the most "deficient" professor at the seminary since the controversial firings back in the 1950s? Secondly, was the process fair? I didn't pull these questions out of thin air. Colleagues had told me that no one had ever been punished like I had been. The term *deficient* came right out of Neal's playbook. The wording was intended to make the committee's work as uncomplicated as possible.

Thus, Jack's response to my written words (as referenced previously) was not only outrageous but sexist to the core. Of course, he began with the standard bromide: "I have pondered and prayed . . . with "a spirit of Christian love." He was a literature professor and he saw a way through his specialty to demean me—to stick it to me one more time: "This melodramatic question may make for good theatre, but melodrama often leaves the audience unsatisfied." Who is the audience here? The committee? Was I supposed to leave them satisfied? Or was Jack, in his supposed cleverness, satisfying an audience of just one—himself?

Lara Rutherford-Morrison sheds light on this and other sexist accusations against women: "that she's being too sensitive, hysterical, or melodramatic." These terms "invalidate and shame a woman." There was no emotion in my written request, but Jack didn't like it so he responded with an emotional and sexist retort. And he would make sure the committee would not allow me to be rated alongside my colleagues because he knew I wouldn't be low on the scale. But Jack was not yet finished with his abuse—abuse of which my colleagues would never learn.

The Battle for my Three-ring Binder

Before the board committee review began, Sid had agreed that the way to proceed was for each side to submit documents. I was relieved. No one had previously wanted to see documents.

After collating them, I added a table of contents and overview and then numbered the pages. I placed them in a large 3-ring binder and submitted them to Jack by the deadline. But Jack was as sly as any villain in a showboat melodrama. Why I trusted him with my documents, I do not know. Within days I received a phone call from him, informing me that the administrators were too busy to collect their documents. He would simply give them copies of mine. I was stunned. Absolutely not. Those were *my* documents and he dare not copy them for the administrators. He had no right to do that. He said he would check back with them. They would have the final word.

My heart was pounding when I got hold of Peter, catching him on the golf course. He took me more seriously than his game and promised to call Jack immediately and tell him he would be in serious legal trouble if he passed on my documents. Days later, two women from the newly formed *ad hoc* committee came to my office to learn why I objected to handing over my documents. One questioned my attitude, wondering why hadn't I moved to Illinois and gotten a full-time position at Trinity where I had previously taught? Had things gone wrong? She suggested the committee should look into it.

I was flabbergasted. I had been thoroughly vetted five years earlier. Fortunately, the other woman appeared to be neutral about my case. She was from outside the CRC. She understood why I had not wanted to leave Grand Rapids as a single mother with a young son in school. And I explained that I had been invited by a Calvin Seminary professor to apply for an open position. As to why I was so protective of my documents, I told them that there were dozens of matters on which opposite claims had been made. I said that the documents would show which side was being truthful. One was unconvinced, the other (neither of whom I knew) agreed that what I was saying made sense. In the end, the administrators had to come up with their own documents.

A Somewhat Fair *Ad Hoc* Committee Report

I had not believed that the *ad hoc* committee would be fair, packed as it was with board members and friends of the seminary. But when the report came out in the summer of 2005, I was surprised that, despite its grasping for ways to defend the administrators, much went in my favor: "We find . . . that "Dr. Tucker would have been better served by a regular two-year reappointment. . . . [W]e do believe that Dr. Tucker merits some form of redress. . . . We recommend that the Board . . . invite the parties to enter into a process of Christian Conciliation to effect a resolution of this matter [with] the authority of mediating the differences." The report also included an addendum which cites "additional deficiencies" in the "reappointment process," including "the use of evaluation forms that are not gender neutral" and "the lack of gender diversity on the Faculty Status Committee." The addendum called on the seminary to "modify evaluation forms to eliminate gender stereotypes."

The committee did not address my alleged "ungodly conduct" and Neal's claim of my thirty-five-minute tirade. That would be left to the "conciliators." But, of course, I had to fight for conciliation, ending up with independent mediators who had no "authority of mediating the differences." They, for example, recommended retroactive pay for me, but had no authority to make it a reality. But the *ad hoc* committee and the mediators did at least offer a path toward justice in my case and for that I am grateful.

I sum up my three plus years with a sports analogy. For two full years, from January of 2003 to the early spring of 2005, I was playing a losing game of defense. But my taking the offense in 2005 was a game changer. I boldly asked for mediation; Henry benched me. I consulted with Peter who passed the ball to Sid. The opposing team sent in Jack. Still on offense, I asked Jack to recuse himself and get out of the game. He refused. I lost yardage with his melodrama, more yardage with his attempted turnover of the binder and to go for the goal. But I caught the fumble, binder safe in my arms and headed down the field. Players piled on. More yardage, back and forth, another first down, and another. The goal in sight and I cross the finish line with independent mediator report tight to my chest. Dancing in the end zone, the whistle blows. Oops! Out of bounds, smudged FAX. Game over.

In 1967 a college student newspaper featured a humorous caption under a picture of a physically-fit young athlete wearing a sleeveless black top, tight black spandex sports pants, hair flying, dashing like a gazelle down a field. A game of flag football. Unaware her flag had been snatched, she just kept going, racing all the way to the end zone. That was me. Perhaps that's a more fitting sports metaphor. The opposing team—Neal, Henry, Duane—had snatched the flag of my dignity, but unaware, I just kept going. And I'm still going as chapter 10 demonstrates.

> You just got fired. Laid off, let go, dismissed, discharged, given a pink slip, booted, sacked, axed, the old heave ho. . . . Whatever the reason, keep things in perspective to transform what appears to be a tragedy into the best thing that ever happened in your career. As you walk down the hallway with a box containing your toilet shaped coffee mug and half-dead spider plant, hold your head high. Let the haters gossip because your boss actually did you a favor. You are on your way to find something better.
>
> Nick Rojas, "Getting Fired: The Best Thing"

A Fired Up Aftermath

Going Public and Celebrating Freedom

I was fired for being gay, and I know what it feels like. I lost everything, but look at me now. I could buy [the Mississippi] governor's mansion, flip it, and make a $7 million profit.

Ellen DeGeneres, April 2016

I felt true relief as I drove my beat-up old green mini-van out of the seminary parking lot for the last time. I had to ask myself why had I fought so hard to stay on when I was being treated so badly. My husband John and I had been married for only two years, and we both looked forward to more peace in our lives. My first response was to go public with a blog. Though written hastily and less lucid than it might have been, I received tens of thousands of hits and hundreds of supportive comments.

Some weeks earlier the religion editor of the *Grand Rapids Press* had contacted me, asking how things were going after six years as the only woman at the seminary. He may have heard rumbles, but that call would be the catalyst for my blog. I knew all too well that media outlets have tight time constraints, and my story could not be told in three minutes. I agreed to get back to him, and his article would be followed by a local TV interview. Board president, Sid Jansma, would become the seminary spokesperson. He insisted that he and the administrators were the most female-affirming folks around.

The Plan that Boomeranged

In his book on academic mobbing, Kenneth Westheus discusses the boomerang effect. The boomerang had hit Neal hard after he learned that I had contacted AAUW with my claim of sex discrimination. The tone of his Mothers' Day letter obviously demonstrated that even though I had a very limited contact with AAUW, he desperately feared being outed. Yet, months later when outside independent mediators were trying frantically to bring some closure to their eight weeks of work with the three administrators and me, the effect of the boomerang was very clear. They had already stated that among other things, I should receive retroactive pay, be appointed full professor and the allegations of ungodly' behavior acknowledged as inflammatory. But I would have had to make a concession as well:

> I most sincerely regret documenting my struggles to Melissa [last name withheld]. I was insensitive to the pain it did cause the people I mentioned by position. The language I used in the letter was provocative and accusatory. I wish I would have been careful and considerate to do nothing that could have harmed their reputations.

The reason for this concession was to give the administrators a few crumbs to balance the pound cake they gave to me. But it was ludicrous to the point of being comical. Why wouldn't I have to apologize for thirty-five minutes of raging vulgarities, as Neal's "notes" indicated? Why not for "scandalizing" the seminary community with "gross misconduct"? Why not? I had given a copy of the letter to Melissa to Peter and said it was fine to pass it on to Neal. I had every right to consult with her—to consult with an attorney, with a counselor or with a member of AAUW. But Neal's demand for this concession reveals how the boomerang come back and hit him hard.

This explains the outrage in his five-page Mothers' Day skreed with repeated references to AAUW. Had he presumed that this was the first time I had spilled the beans beyond the seminary? As a matter of fact, I had been spilling beans all along. In fact, I had sought advice from anyone who might be able to help me. My letter to Melissa amounted to almost nothing by comparison. If that futile communication to AAUW boomeranged and was the "cause" of "pain" and "harmed their reputations," how much greater must have been the publication of my blog? I was told that it created *chaos* at the seminary

Blogging "My Calvin Seminary Story"

During my time at the seminary, personal blogging was coming into its own, and by the time I left in late August of 2006, I was ready to launch my story. I had a ready-made audience, and many seminary students contacted me with support. Colleagues were silent. In the midst of the *chaos,* the administrators were trying to keep a lid on things—except for gossip of my "ungodliness." But my blog did prompt passionate responses, as this sampling indicates:

Male head of a Grand Rapids ministry: "I've read through your story at the link below. You've been through a wrenching experience and I respect you more than ever for handling it as you have. I think you're right to stand your ground."

Seminary student of mine: [My wife] "and I have both said from the time we set foot on campus at CTS that there is an "aura of suspicion there. If you're not like everyone else, then you must be in the wrong (maybe even "ungodly"?). . . . I am 100% with you on this garbage of using the 'confidential' label so you do not have to give details and can make some kind of accusation or recommendation without any real basis. . . . But to pull out a bunch of worthless red herrings that they can't even defend as close to the truth, that is just plain wrong."

Male head of a large Pasadena ministry: "I read every word. . . . I am sure this is a blow. CTS is also damaged. They have shot themselves in the foot. I am terribly sorry. Yours is a chapter in the growing up of the CRC."

Male corporate executive from Washington state with Princeton Seminary connections: "Got it, read it. Will fw it to as many as I can."

Seminary married students: "We're thinking of you and your sad experience with CTS. Thank you for sharing this with us, as painful as it may be for you. Receive our sympathy and love."

Leading male CRC administrator: "Be sure that you know some of the rest of us are also saddened by your evident pain and continuing distress. Someday I may want to share with you my own story of what some would call my "marginalization" by Calvin Seminary.

Previous administrator at seminary: "Thank you for alerting me to your 'blog.' It is done with graceful forthrightness. Your sense of pain at believing you were done grievous injustice is palpable, but I do not sense any vindictiveness in your statement. I have always admired and appreciated you as a colleague. Thanks for your fine contributions to education at

Calvin Seminary. My very best wishes for you and John in all your future endeavors."

Long-time female seminary staff member: "Reading through it just quickly brings back the sadness and hurt you have had to endure for so long."

Female seminary student: "I just read your blog and don't have adequate words to say how sorry I am for what you've gone through and how appalled I am at what the CTS administrators have done. . . . This is so devastating for you and for the school as a whole. I, too, am sad that students won't get to learn from you and be forced to think by you! Your ability to present material and challenge students to address the gray areas of theology and ministry are such a gift and these are needed in a denomination that has the tendency to hide behind cut and dried theology. Oh how my heart hurts for you."

Male seminary student: "It's clear you've been having an awful time in the past year! I had no idea. It sounds like much of this was in process even while I was in your Missions History class. Again, I was clueless to your turmoil. What a heavy burden you must have been carrying the whole time! How lonely! It sounds very difficult and very messy. I'm so sorry."

Female Fuller Seminary professor: "I missed you at Techny this year and wondered what had happened. I'm very sorry for what you have endured. You'll always be a hero to me."

Long-time CRC minister: "I would hope that WVD did not partake in this charade at CTS. His daughter is a provost at Western Seminary. He is a seminary classmate of mine."

Male CRC church member: "I am taking this opportunity to let you know that I am appalled that so-called Godly men have mishandled/mistreated you at the Sem. . . . I just want you to know that I support, or am behind you 100%."

Female seminary graduate: "What a story. I'm saddened to know that you experienced such injustice (and hurt) and also by knowing how systematic such abuse can be. I sent the link on to quite a few members."

Male seminary professor from the Netherlands: "The most astonishing point is, of course, your testimony to what happened at Calvin. . . .I really am very proud of your great courage in this regard. You must have a very strong spirit, because a lot of people would not be able to cope stress after stress."

Male graduate of seminary: "I grieve with you over the events of the past three years. I would add that these events, in my opinion, did not affect your professionalism nor your fine interaction with students. I have been most grateful for your friendship and encouragement since I came to CTS in 2003. Thank you for encouraging me in my calling and in my studies!"

Husband/wife professors and authors: "[We] just spent an hour reading it and some of the related material, and talking about it. As veterans of the Christian academic world our first response is 'no surprise' and yet, dear God, 'surprise' indeed."

Female professor at Calvin College: "Dear Ruth--wow. What a story. It is so sad to me to hear about this kind of treatment of you--again and in detail--and I can't help but think it is indeed gender related. I am so sad for you, the seminary, and the CRC. This whole set of events is a blot on the church."

Former male seminary student: "I had heard the "mutterings" but I did not know the actual story. I am so sorry about what happened."

Professor at Trinity Evangelical Divinity School: "I am . . . appalled and so sorry. You are a good teacher and a good Christian. I cannot imagine the pain and suffering you have endured through this. I'll write more later after I return. I am grieving for you."

Former male seminary student: "I am disappointed in my seminary, in leaders who I had respected and looked up to. I don't know what else to say, except that this is a very sad part of the seminary's story. For what it's worth, I thought you were one of the better professors I had -- during my time at CTS. I enjoyed our class discussions, and I particularly remember your hospitality that one Thursday morning on the Grand River."

Female in the CRC: "I just read your sad story. The mistake was made by the administration, in Jan. 2003. Not acknowledging that mistake is the problem. The rest is consequence. It is a crime against humanity, first, that this was done to you, and second, that a mistake by others has put you in a position to have to defend yourself to such great lengths. I know of all the issues: fortress mentality of administration, code of silence, confidentiality smoke screen, gender bias, community confusion, community distancing, etc. I know everything about blaming the victim."

Former male seminary student: "I just heard about what happened and I wanted to send an email and just say that I felt sick as I read what you've gone through over the past years. . . . I am so sorry you have had to endure all this. I enjoyed you both as a professor and as someone to talk to around the seminary.

New female seminary student: "I just started at this CTS this fall in the MTS program. I read your book *Walking Away from Faith* a couple of years ago--in the midst of a three-year struggle over whether or not to go to seminary—and it had a profound impact on me. . . . What I really want to say is that I am grieved to read about what has happened to you, and I am sure that it is a great loss to my education. I would have liked very much to have been in your class."

Former Calvin College student to a minister: "VERY sad news. I can relate somewhat with what Ruth went through at CTS. . . . it parallels very closely with my own experience at Calvin College. On Calvin, I've moved on and healed. Let me just say that "institutional racism" is alive and well at Calvin, as is sexism at CTS."

West Michigan man: "I read with great concern the article in the Grand Rapids press. [I have] concern primarily for what this account does for the name of Jesus Christ. . . . It does great harm to the name of Jesus in the public square. . . . Thank you for not taking your case to the courts since this is prohibited by the Bible. . . . I am glad however, that I won't have to answer to him on judgement day for taking a matter like this public.

Male seminary graduate: "I'm overwhelmed and terribly saddened to hear of your loneliness over the years, and of course the injustices meted [out] to you. Your situation is something I was not aware of, and I'm ashamed for not inquiring or noticing. Ruth, I am sorry to be part of a system which has so insulted you. I will reflect, also with friends in ministry, what your experience means for us in the CRC."

No Regrets

Despite the terrible treatment meted out to me by the administrators, I do not regret the ordeal—no more than I regret marrying a serial abuser in 1968, as I have written in *Black and White Bible, Black and Blue Wife*. Without that union I would not have my son or granddaughter. The same goes for the abusive hounding me out of the seminary. Without those painful years, would I have become friends with Myra Kraker? She had endured hostility from supervisors at Calvin College. When my minister's wife learned what I was going through, she said, *you've got to get together with Myra.* We connected and discovered we were, dare I say, *soul mates.* The hostility she was enduring, however, had an additional ominous component.

Myra was terminally ill with pancreatic cancer. We talked about that side of her life, but she was in remission and stubbornly behaved as though she was doing fine. She had bad days, however, and on one late afternoon she learned about a hastily-called departmental meeting for the next morning. She got out of her sick bed, went to the meeting only to learn that the department head had rearranged her course schedule without consulting her—forcing her to reschedule doctors' appointments and meetings with colleagues from other institutions. She had collegial friends, but was treated badly by a department head and administrators. Like me, she would not have been considered a sweet, submissive, subdued godly lady. She spoke her mind, and that was one of the reasons I loved her as a dear friend and colleague.

Myra would die of her terrible disease. Besides family and dozens of dear friends, she was survived by her beloved husband, John Worst, to whom she was married for less than four years. She had told me that, despite her terminal illness, her years with him had been the happiest of her life. I had become acquainted with John through her—and the rest is history. No regrets.

October in Italy

Knowing months earlier that my days at the seminary were numbered, I had accepted an opportunity to travel to a tiny town in Italy to teach a short course in October. It was a wonderful time for John and me to get away and forget the turmoil back home. From my online journal: "Greeting from San Lorenzo":

> Yesterday, after an uneventful flight, we arrived in this sleepy old-world village about an hour from Venice. It's a little foretaste of heaven, at least that's John's perspective after tasting the local wine. Our loft bedroom overlooks wine country as far as the eye can see. We're enjoying the delicious Italian food in the dining hall that opens to the wonderful stone courtyard, flowers and palm trees under blue skies. Much of this afternoon we biked along narrow roads in the countryside through corn fields and vineyards, stopping by the town of Valvasone which sports a wonderful medieval castle and narrow stone streets bordered by ancient houses tightly bound one to another. So far, T-shirt weather. Tomorrow, the work begins--team-teaching a course to

American College students: "Memoirs: Reading and Writing the Stories of Our Lives."

Fewer than twenty students in the class, it was one of the most emotionally-charged courses I have ever taught. I pushed them like I'd never pushed students before. On the final afternoon when they were summarizing and quoting from their stories, one student said she had finally come to terms with her sister's death. As she told the class about her sister's suicide, she said that she had talked with her mother the night before and for the first time acknowledged that the suicide was not her own fault—terrible guilt she had suffered for several years.

An Unemployed Professor

Within months after I was gone from the seminary, I applied for unemployment benefits, assuming it would be an open and shut case. Far from it. The Seminary would counter with its attorneys. Although the State of Michigan was the entity sending the checks, the seminary was required to pay into the fund. I served as my own attorney, quoting from documents showing the hostile environment and sex discrimination. I won and would receive checks for more than a year.

At the same time, I was contacting nearby seminaries and colleges seeking a teaching position. Nothing. Had I been blacklisted? A man had written a friend of mine, criticizing me for going public: "[I]n the end it will hurt her. Any prospective employer has to be thinking: 'Here's trouble coming, trouble we don't need.'" He was right. The fear of being blacklisted stops professors dead in their tracks, as Kenneth Westhues explains: "Many academics cooperate in a cover-up because they are ashamed . . . [and] are not accustomed to seeking publicity. . . . This means that if discreet efforts are made to get rid of them, many are inclined to go quietly. For them, going public is not dignified."

People sometimes asked if I were bitter. I wasn't. Nine months after leaving the seminary, June 1 2007, I wrote in my online journal:

I'm happier now than I've ever been. It's the absolute best time of my life—except that I'm WAY too busy with writing and speaking. Since I left CTS last August 31, I've taught a course in Italy, had 2 women's retreats in Japan, have lectured in Texas twice, in Indiana, in Grand Rapids several times (have 2 pastors' retreats coming up in Minneapolis and Palm Springs in the next 2 months), an interview on one of my books with FOX news next week, and am trying to complete 2 book contracts. John Worst is an absolutely wonderful husband; we bike and canoe and hike and travel for fun. I am so incredibly glad I'm out of CTS.

More Trouble at the Seminary

The most significant event that happened at the seminary since I left involved another colleague. While I was still there, he had been chosen by the faculty to be our representative overseeing a routine evaluation of Neal. All faculty and staff were asked to submit evaluations. After I left the seminary, I learned that this colleague was told he was being let go. The official reason was cost-cutting. The real reason, I was told, was because he had wanted Neal's evaluation to be taken seriously by the board. Unlike me he was a tenured professor and an insider—a *good old boy*. The faculty rallied around and saved his job. I have no documents to support this time of turmoil, though I do know it was a very painful ordeal for him. He was a friend (on sabbatical when I was fired) who had treated me kindly. In October of 2009, three years after I was hounded out of the seminary, I wrote in my journal:

> I was out of town with no online access today and yesterday and got home to emails from Calvin Seminary sources. It seems that Neal Plantinga . . . is on his way out. There's a story behind it, but he says publicly: "I have prayed earnestly about this decision and have made it freely and joyfully."

The three-man administration would be history by the summer of 2010. One administrator, beneath the top three, would express to me in person, his relief, saying: "It's been a wasted decade." One year later, the seminary administrator who had hired me was biking past my shop and stopped by to chat. "He told me," quoting from my journal, "that the faculty was very excited now to be getting a new president---that the school has been dropping in enrollment for the past 5 years." Then I added in my journal: "I take no credit for that but my tenure there ended exactly 5 years ago this week."

Larycia Hawkins and Wheaton College

In January of 2016, after Larycia's story had been picked up by hundreds of media outlets, I wrote about her situation on my online journal: "Now it's being reported that Wheaton College faculty council has unanimously voted that the recommendation to have her 'tenure and employment terminated' be withdrawn. It seems that the biggest issue at the moment is process—an unfair, inept and biased process."

I could have wished that my tenured colleagues had defended me like that. Our situations, however, were very different. She had previously been required to reaffirm the school's statement of faith because she had said things that were deemed controversial. A black woman speaking boldly about how badly minorities were treated, she was thought to be too liberal for Wheaton constituents. Then during the advent season in 2015, after widely publicized attacks on Muslim communities, she donned a hijab to show her support. On her Facebook, she wrote: "I stand in religious solidarity with Muslims because they, like me, a Christian, are people of the book. And as Pope Francis stated last week, we worship the same God."

As controversial as that sounded to many Evangelicals, some came to her defense from a cultural standpoint. Explaining the Christian faith to Muslims, missionaries routinely use Allah when speaking of God. And, in fact, a colleague from Trinity Evangelical Divinity School where I had taught, defended her on that point. But action was taken very quickly by Wheaton administrators. In February, less than two months after her Facebook eruption, the two parties announced a parting of the ways, having "reached a confidential agreement.".

Larycia would accept a teaching fellowship at the University of Virginia, followed by a series of one-year appointments, supplemented by speaking engagements. But the ordeal, not surprisingly, took a serious toll. Some four years later she confided how she was still "experiencing mental trauma and anxiety and depression." Just when she needed support, she had begun a new career a thousand miles away, which was indeed "hard on [her] relationship with friends and family."

Wheaton College appeared to weather the storm, carrying on as it had done before. Like administrators from so many other Christian schools, they prayed about their decision, pacified their constituents, and paid for a silencing clause.

Trauma, Anxiety, Depression

The pain that Larycia endured in the years following her Wheaton dismissal is all too common among those who are fired. It might be assumed that a highly capable young professor could easily find another position, but the black-listing of *Here comes trouble* is real. Short-term opportunities arise, but in a tough academic job market it's not simple to find a comparable fulfilling position. Larycia stands out in that she has publicly shared the trauma, anxiety, depression that at times seemed almost overwhelming. Sheri Klouda relocated with her little family, accepted a lower salary and benefits package (much needed for her husband's underlying health issues) all the while paying a mortgage on a home that didn't sell easily in a down market. All in all, a very painful ordeal, particularly so when she was assessed costs upon losing her court case against the abusive and wealthy Paige Patterson.

It is painful to read the stories of others who have suffered far more than I have. In fact, I consider myself fortunate to have weathered the storm and can now write about it much more dispassionately than when the wounds were still so raw.

There is a lot of good advice out there about increasing resilience. Here, I want to focus on the remarkable benefits of sharing your story. Emotional, autobiographical storytelling can be a path to truly owning your story. Further, by "giving it away," you can use your own journey as a means to help others on theirs.

Sherry Hamby, "Resilience and Benefits to Sharing Your Story"

A Final Word

As I write, it's now nearly fifteen years since I've been away from the seminary. John and I still live in a flood plain on the Grand River seven miles north of Grand Rapids. We've weathered many floods, including the 100-year flood of 2013, giving us some celebrity when the front page of the *Grand Rapids Press* featured a photograph of the two of us kayaking down our road with water up to the mailboxes. We've come to love the River and the life it offers, but we no longer hoist our kayaks two at a time so easily as we head to the dozen steps down to the water. We feel our age. No more days of 50-mile biking, no more water-skiing. Even our hiking is curtailed. We still drive south in January to Big Bend National Park on the Rio Grande in Texas (except during a pandemic). But we no longer take a chance on the most rigorous trails.

John is now eighty, and I'm five years behind. We do, however, maintain our little shop, founded in 1996, a hobby too personal to give up. We have help from family members when we really need it, but on most days we're there alone when customers wander in. It's located on an acre of land just a block south of the Grand Rapids border, on a busy five-lane road. We do not advertise, fearing hordes of people, and we have no inclination to hire workers.

Guests comment that they've never seen such a delightful shop. I would say the same were I to happen on it by chance. Besides the house (as it once was) with its big wrap-around porch and other additions, there are twenty out-buildings, some very small but all open and containing product: Apple House, Percy's shed, play house, Olde Junk Shoppe, Breton Cottage, red barn, cabin, coop, stable, bird house, Chapel by the Bridge, Mexico House, Wash House, Garden House, Up-north Barn, tiki hut, sign shop, statuary shed, Christmas House, potting shed, and outhouse—all displaying my iconic outdoor folk-art painted on various mediums, items that are often purchased but mainly copied with my compliments, as the signs say: "Snap a picture, Make your own." Also onsite, gazebos, pergolas, vine structures, picnic tables, outdoor seating, ponds, waterfalls, woodland garden, gnome village, totem pole garden, a ten-foot windmill, butterfly arch, all joined by walkways and rock gardens. It's a wonderfully enchanting place to spend our senior years.

Self-Pity and Laughter

Writing about his ten-year old self and the loss of his father by suicide, Fredrick Buechner concludes: "I hear the self-pity in that, but I do not apologize for it. I pity the child who happens to be me the way I would pity any child under similar circumstances." As I write this book, like Buechner, I have the distance in looking back. I pity that confident woman who was brought so low on that dark, late January afternoon in Henry's office. I pity her as I would pity any woman in such circumstances even as I'm struggling to recognize her. Who was this woman so terribly humiliated that her last best option was a groveling question: *Does anyone have to know?* I hardly know her, but she has my pity.

Pity, but also laughter. Last night, as I was writing this, I pulled out a document that I had not recently seen. I read a sentence to myself, then read it aloud to John sitting nearby. I read it still again and we started laughing. It was so over the top that it struck us both as absurdly funny. The background to the document was my utter frustration in 2003. As I related it previously, I had said to a colleague that no one pays a speck of attention to my problem and that I'd come to my wits end. And then I facetiously said that I might as well [as I couched it] run through the halls naked and jump off the bell tower. Then they would pay attention.

What we laughed at was the sheer lunacy of the administrators' summary for the Ad Hoc committee two years later in 2005. Under a centered heading in bold print, "2004 Facts," there were two short paragraphs of facts relating to my sabbatical, my improved student evaluations, and board members reporting "positively" on class visits. Mixed in with the good was the bad, my having written once that I was "too busy" and again that I was "swamped."

Then came the third paragraph and my flippant threat: "But in March of 2003 Professor Tucker lapsed into reprehensible conduct and scandalized members of the faculty and staff by it." Now fifteen years later, we were laughing at the absurdity of it. Had my co-workers actually been scandalized by imagining me naked, or was it my jumping off the tower? As far as I recall, there were only three of them who knew about this "reprehensible conduct"—unless the administrators had spread the word to the whole community. Whatever. At least it gave John and me a good laugh as we re-read the document.

What If? Imagining a Different Scenario

I've always liked to think in counterfactuals. *What if* things had happened differently? What if Henry had looked over student evaluation statistics of *all* of the faculty members and had noted that there was room for improvement? What if he had distributed a copy of blank student evaluations for each of us at a faculty meeting and suggested we all pay more attention to it, pointing out that the evaluation form had not come out of thin air. When formulated, it was mindful of founder John Calvin, the three confessions, the Bible and even some pedagogical basics. For those of us who found this suggestion to be a sudden flash of insight, his short pep talk might have made a big difference. *What if* all faculty were encouraged to raise their student evaluations, rather than damning just one for her *deficits*?

What if Neal during a fall faculty retreat had offered a session on the topic he professed to know so well: *godliness*, pointing out that there was not enough of it among the faculty? What if he had appointed as *seminary elders* five tenured faculty-room regulars (John, John, Arie, Cal and Richard) to be in charge of the *faculty room ethos*? If anyone were to get *out of line*, they would kindly encourage the offender to get back in line. *What if* those five had been graciously chosen instead of suggesting the woman, new to the seminary, fill that role?

And what if the woman professor had not been singled out to be terminated? What if she had been permitted to continue on tenure track and was appointed full professor? What if she had announced in a faculty meeting in the early autumn of 2009 that, after a decade of teaching, she was retiring—that the spring term would be her last? And, what if she had been surprised when she came to the faculty lunch room in May of 2010 with a fine catered lunch, all her colleagues making kind remarks, but mainly kidding and laughing about the good times they'd had with her? *What if?*

Closure

People have asked, "Have you had any sense of closure?" It's difficult to have closure in a case like mine when there are no apologies. The administrators would carry on in their positions, their reputations unscathed. A heart-felt public apology would not allow them, as already mentioned, to *save face.* Perhaps someday, however, an apology will be offered. Larry Gara comes to mind. Fired in 1962 from the Grove City College (a Presbyterian school in Pennsylvania), he had never expected an apology.

Gara was controversial before coming to the school. A Quaker and conscientious objector, he spent three years in federal prison during World War II, and after his release was incarcerated a second time for helping a student apply for CO status. Behind bars, he couldn't be silenced, on one occasion protesting the racist practice of barring black inmates from the mess hall where white convicts ate. Out of prison, he studied hard and capped off his education with a PhD from the University of Wisconsin. He taught for five years before he was fired, having been accused of several infractions, some supported by faculty colleagues—and by students who deemed his grading too hard. Other professors defended him, one saying he was the "most competent teacher barring none that we have ever had on the campus." Another referred to him as one of the school's "intellectual ornaments."

But the president and the board president decided to give the boot to this controversial history professor—and "communist." A footnote to the story is that those responsible for the firing were closely tied to the John Birch Society. That fact and questionable protocol prompted an alumnus of the school to dig into the case some five decades later. His published account led to a public apology in 2015, fifty-three years after the firing, when the surprised Gara was ninety-three years old.

So, I'm holding out for a public apology, hopefully not having to wait more than a half century. And it would perhaps come most appropriately from board President Sid Jansma, who would have some things in common with Grove City board president J. Howard Pew, both wealthy oilmen who gave of their wealth to the school they served.

Of course, Sid would no doubt say that I'm telling only one side of the story—as would the administrators. Of course. In fact, Neal accused me of doing just that when I had summarized my case for Melissa of AAUW. But, as the outside mediators stated, my case is well-documented. In an era when *alternative facts* are deemed just as valid as *facts*, documents do indeed matter.

My former colleagues could also step up to the plate and apologize. Had they joined together and stood by me in my demand that the evidence against me be opened up, they could have saved my job. I've seen many of them since. They have greeted me kindly. But not one of them has said how sorry he is that he personally and the whole faculty failed me. None have said: *You deserved better from us.* None have said: *Some of us would like to get together with you and try to bring some closure.* There's still time.

NOTES

A Short Explanation

I t is odd for an academic not to have extensive notes. Indeed, I've formulated more reference notes during my career of writing books and scholarly articles than I could possibly account for. There are no such notes (except for these "Notes") in this volume for a number of reasons.

- By self-publishing, no one is forcing me to do so.
- This book is in part dependent on memories that cannot be documented.
- Most of the material I cite is from unpublished emails, letters and memos.
- Outside information is easily found online.

Let me explain, with the help of a little Latin.[1] The temporary disappointment of having my partial manuscript rejected by a publisher has accrued some benefits for me. At least that is how I've remained optimistic and avoided the temptation to submit the manuscript elsewhere. It has also given me boundless liberty in my writing.

Destitutus ventis, remos adhibe.[2]

---

1. These Latin quotations are accessible online; they are not a product of my unreliable memory from eighth-grade Latin.
2. Should the wind fail, use the oars.

This volume is at least a partial memoir. In *Unreliable Truth: On Memoir and Memory*, Maureen Murdock underscores the fickle nature of memory. I fully agree. In fact, time and again as I was writing, my memory was faulty—nearly always in a tempered fashion. I had nearly forgotten how awful those years had been for me. But my memory swiftly returned as I began re-reading the documents, and now many years later the truth they tell no longer stings.

Forsan et haec olim meminisse iuvabit.[3]

As I have previously stated, my case is document rich. In other such stories that I've read online or listened to in person, there has never been so much documentation—absolutely never. That is one reason why my case is so significant. Memory simply cannot prove what documents can, and the vast majority of my documents are from the very administrators who forced me out of the seminary. After this volume is published, I will have a copy of the documents available—if I can convince the archives department (Heritage Hall) at the Hekman Library of Calvin University to hold them. This would not be an outlandish request. Among other things, according to the website,"the collection holds the personal papers of the university and seminary faculty."

In absentia lucis, tenebrae vincunt.[4]

Most of the other material cited in this book can easily be accessed online. So the reader is on her own. Type or cut and paste a partial quote on google and it should come right up. I tried to hunt down books, but they simply haven't been written. True, there is *Administrative Mobbing of High Achieving Professors* and other volumes by Kenneth Westhues, but they also are largely available online. This volume is thus both a reliable memoir and reliable history.

Finis coronat opus.[5]

3. This suffering will yield as yet a pleasant tale to tell (John Conington, 1866 translation).
4. In the absence of light, darkness prevails (*Washington Post* motto).
5. The end crowns the work.